••• **Louise Hashemi and Barbara Thomas**

IELTS
TRAINER

SIX PRACTICE TESTS
WITHOUT ANSWERS

CAMBRIDGE
UNIVERSITY PRESS

University Printing House, Cambridge CB2 8BS, United Kingdom

Cambridge University Press is part of the University of Cambridge.

It furthers the University's mission by disseminating knowledge in the pursuit of education, learning and research at the highest international levels of excellence.

www.cambridge.org
Information on this title: www.cambridge.org/9780521171106

© Cambridge University Press 2011

First published 2011

A catalogue record for this publication is available from the British Library

ISBN 978-0-521-17110-6 Practice Tests
ISBN 978-0-521-12820-9 Practice Tests with Answers and Audio CDs (3)
ISBN 978-0-521-18707-7 Audio CDs (3)

Contents

Introduction

What is IELTS?

The International English Language Testing System (IELTS) is widely recognised as a test of language ability of candidates who need to study or work where English is the language of communication.

There are two types of IELTS test: the Academic Module (taken for entry to undergraduate or postgraduate studies or for professional reasons) and the General Training Module (taken for entry to vocational or training programmes not at degree level, for admission to secondary schools and for immigration purposes). Both modules are made up of four parts – Listening, Reading, Writing and Speaking. The Listening and Speaking tests are the same for both Academic and General Training but the Reading and Writing tests are different.

Who is IELTS Trainer for?

This book is suitable for anyone who is preparing to take the International English Language Testing System (IELTS) Academic Module. IELTS Trainer can be used in class with a teacher, or – in the case of the with-answers edition of the book – by students working on their own at home. It is aimed at candidates who would like to achieve a Band Score of 6 or higher. (See section on Scoring below.)

What is IELTS Trainer?

This book contains six practice tests for IELTS, each covering the Listening, Reading, Writing and Speaking papers. The practice tests in Guided Tests 1 and 2 are also accompanied by training and advice. All six tests are at the level of the exam.

In Test 1 each part of each paper consists of a training section and an exam practice section:

- The training sections have information and exercises to help you prepare for each part of the paper. In the Listening, Writing and Speaking papers, Test 1 presents and practises grammar, vocabulary and functional language relevant to those papers. This is supported by work on correcting common errors made by IELTS candidates in the exam, as shown by the Cambridge Learner Corpus (see below). In Writing, there are extracts from the scripts of IELTS candidates as well as model answers.

- The exam practice sections consist of the test itself accompanied by step-by-step guidance for each task with tips on strategy and advice linked to the questions. There is a wide range of tasks in the IELTS Listening and Reading papers and the same task may not always appear in the same part of the exam every time. The practice tests reflect this variety and training is given in Tests 1 and 2 in all the major task types which you will come across.

Test 2 contains training for the exam focusing on the task types not covered in Test 1, in addition to a review of information in Test 1. The training sections are shorter in Test 2 than in Test 1. Test 2 also contains an exam practice section with tips and advice on how to deal with the practice test itself.

Tests 3–6 are complete practice tests without advice or training. They contain variations of the task types in Tests 1 and 2 and cover a wide range of topics and text types. They give you the opportunity to practise the strategies and skills you have acquired while working through Tests 1 and 2.

There is an Explanatory answer key (see below) for each test in the with-answers edition.

How to use *IELTS Trainer*

Test 1 Training

- For each part of the paper (e.g. Listening Section 1, page 10), first read the overview **What is ...?**, describing the type(s) of task which that part may contain. For some parts there is also a section called **What does it test?** which describes, for example, the kind of skills that part of the exam tests (e.g. identifying key facts, understanding speakers' opinions).

- Read through the **Task information** which describes in detail the particular task type that follows.

- Look at the information marked **Tip!** which gives general advice on exam strategy and language.

- Work through **Useful language** exercises in the Listening, Writing and Speaking sections before tackling the exam tasks on the practice pages. These training exercises help to develop the necessary skills and offer practice directly relevant to the exam tasks in Test 1. Answers to the exercises are in the **Explanatory answer key** (see below). Many exercises involve focusing on and correcting common language mistakes made by actual IELTS candidates, as shown by the **Cambridge Learner Corpus** (see below).

- Check the boxes marked **Advice**. These give practical help with individual questions.

- In **Listening**, use one of the numbered **CDs**, e.g. 01. A CD player (or a computer that plays CDs) is required.

- In Test 1 **Writing**, many exercises are based on language used in IELTS essays in the **Cambridge Learner Corpus** and sample answers written by actual IELTS candidates, as well as model answers which show what is expected of the best candidates. The **Explanatory answer key** contains answers to the exercises. These training exercises build up to an exam task at the end which is similar to, but not the same as, those in the training exercises.

- In **Speaking**, there are exercises which build into a bank of personalised, useful language for the first part of the test and other exercises which practise the language necessary for the prepared talk and discussion which follow in Parts 2 and 3. These can be used with a partner, or working alone, for timed practice.

Test 1 Exam practice

- Read the **Action plan** for each task in the Listening, Reading and Writing papers immediately before working through the exam practice task. There are many different task types and the Action plans show how to approach each type in the best way to achieve good marks and avoid wasting time.

- Work through the task, carefully following the steps of the Action plan and making use of the help in the **Tip!** information and **Advice** boxes.

- Answers to all items are in the **Explanatory answer key**, which explains why the correct answers are right and others are wrong. For Listening, the parts of the **Transcripts** which give the correct answers are underlined.

Test 2 Training

- Answer the questions in the **Review** section to remind yourself about each part of the test. If you need to, use the cross-reference to Test 1 to check your answers.

- Work through the exercises in the Writing and Speaking sections. The Speaking section extends the strategies and skills introduced in Test 1 and adds to the topics which you might be asked about. The Writing section revises the strategies covered in Test 1 and offers further targeted language training exercises. Many of the exercises are based on IELTS candidates' answers from the Cambridge Learner Corpus.

Test 2 Exam practice

- Answer the questions in each **Action plan reminder**. These ask you about strategies which were introduced in Test 1. Use the cross-reference to refer back to Test 1 if you need to.

- Read through the **Action plans** for the new task types which weren't in Test 1. Use the **Tip!** information and **Advice** boxes to help you do the tasks and the **Explanatory answer key** to check your answers.

Tests 3–6 Exam practice

- Try to do the exam tasks under exam conditions where possible, applying the skills and language learnt in Guided Tests 1 and 2.

- For the Speaking paper, it is better to work with a partner so that you can ask each other the questions. If that is not possible, follow the instructions and do all three parts alone. Use a watch and keep to the correct time. Recording the test and listening to it can help you identify language areas which need more practice.

You can do Tests 3–6 in any order, but you should always try to keep to the time recommended for each paper.

The Cambridge Learner Corpus (CLC)

The Cambridge Learner Corpus (CLC) is a large collection of exam scripts written by students taking Cambridge ESOL English exams around the world. It currently contains over 85,000 scripts and is growing all the time. It forms part of the Cambridge International Corpus (CIC) and it has been built up by Cambridge University Press and Cambridge ESOL. The CLC currently contains scripts from over:

- 85,000 students
- 100 different first languages
- 180 different countries

Exercises and extracts from candidates' answers from Writing in *IELTS Trainer* which are based on the CLC are indicated by this icon: ⊙

Other components of *IELTS Trainer*

- The **Explanatory answer key** on pages 173–231 of the with-answers edition gives the correct answers, and explains them where necessary (especially in Tests 1 and 2). In some cases, such as multiple-choice questions, it also explains why the other possible answers are wrong.

- The full **Transcripts** for the Listening paper are given in the with-answers edition, with the parts of the transcript that give the correct answers underlined.

- **Answer sheets** for the Reading and Listening papers are at the back of the book. Before you take the exam, you should study these so that you know how to mark or write your answers correctly. In Writing, the question paper has plenty of lined space for you to write your answers.

- **3 audio CDs** contain recordings for the Listening papers of the six IELTS tests. The listening material is indicated by a different icon in *IELTS Trainer* for each of the CDs: 🎧 01 🎧 01 🎧 01

International English Language Testing System (IELTS)

Level of IELTS

You do not pass or fail IELTS. You get a Band Score between 1 and 9. Candidates scoring 9 have fluent, accurate English, with wide-ranging vocabulary, making very few errors and will be capable of performing in English in professional and academic contexts. Candidates scoring 7 can understand and communicate effectively in English, using some complex language, and although there may be errors, these do not impede communication. A score of 5 or lower means that the candidate has a limited range of language and that errors in grammar, pronunciation, etc. lead to misunderstandings.

Different organisations and institutions publish the Band Score they require for entry.

Scoring

The **Listening Test** contains 40 items and each correct item is given one mark.

The **Reading Test** contains 40 items and each correct item is given one mark. The Academic and General Training Reading Tests are graded to the same level. However, because the texts in the Academic Reading Test are more challenging overall than those in the General Training Test, more questions need to be answered correctly on a General Training Test to receive the same grade.

The **Writing Test** (both Academic and General Training) is marked on the following areas: Task Achievement (for Task 1), Task Response (for Task 2), Coherence and Cohesion, Lexical Resource, Grammatical Range and Accuracy. Examiners give a Band Score for each of these criteria, which are equally weighted.

For the **Speaking Test**, a Band Score is given for each of the following which are equally weighted: Fluency and Coherence, Lexical Resource, Grammatical Range and Pronunciation.

Candidates receive scores on a Band Scale from 1 to 9 for each skill tested (Listening, Reading, Writing and Speaking). They are of equal importance. These four scores are then averaged and rounded to produce an Overall Band Score. Each candidate receives a Test Report Form setting out their Overall Band Score and their scores for each test. The scores are reported in whole bands or half bands according to the nine-band score given below.

If you do the practice tests in *IELTS Trainer* under exam conditions, you need to score approximately 20 marks on both the Reading and Listening Test for a Band Score of around 5.5. To achieve a Band Score of 7, you need approximately 30 marks on Reading and Listening.

IELTS Band Scores

9 Expert user – Has fully operational command of the language: appropriate, accurate and fluent with complete understanding.

8 Very good user – Has fully operational command of the language with only occasional unsystematic inaccuracies and inappropriacies. Misunderstandings may occur in unfamiliar situations. Handles complex detailed argumentation well.

7 Good user – Has operational command of the language, though with occasional inaccuracies, inappropriacies and misunderstandings in some situations. Generally handles complex language well and understands detailed reasoning.

6 Competent user – Has generally effective command of the language despite some inaccuracies, inappropriacies and misunderstandings. Can use and understand fairly complex language, particularly in familiar situations.

5 Modest user – Has partial command of the language, coping with overall meaning in most situations, though is likely to make many mistakes. Should be able to handle basic communication in own field.

4 Limited user – Basic competence is limited to familiar situations. Has frequent problems in understanding and expression. Is not able to use complex language.

3 Extremely limited user – Conveys and understands only general meaning in very familiar situations. Frequent breakdowns in communication occur.

2 Intermittent user – No real communication is possible except for the most basic information using isolated words or short formulae in familiar situations and to meet immediate needs. Has great difficulty understanding spoken and written English.

1 Non-user – Essentially has no ability to use the language beyond possibly a few isolated words.

0 Did not attempt the test – No assessable information provided.

For more information on grading and results, go to the Cambridge ESOL website (see below).

Content of IELTS

IELTS has four papers, each consisting of 2, 3 or 4 parts. For details on each part, see the tables below.

Paper 1 Listening about 30 minutes, with 10 minutes to transfer answers to the answer sheet at the end

- This paper is common to both the Academic and General Training Modules.
- The topics in Parts 1 and 2 are based around social situations but the topics in Parts 3 and 4 are all in an educational or training context.
- The **level of difficulty** increases from Section 1 to Section 4.
- Each section is heard **once only**.
- The **instructions** for each task are on the question paper.
- There is a short **pause** before each section which can be used to look at the task and questions. Where there is more than one task in a section, there is also a short pause before the part of the recording which relates to the next task.
- A brief introductory explanation of the **context** is heard before each section, but is **not** printed on the question paper.
- **At the end** of the Listening test there are ten minutes to copy answers onto the answer sheet.
- Correct **spelling** is essential on the answer sheet.

	No. of questions	Text type	Task types *Each section has one or more of these tasks.*	Task information
1	10	a conversation or interview between two speakers, giving and exchanging information about an everyday topic	completing notes	pages 10, 67
			completing a form	page 61
			completing a table	pages 21, 62
2	10	a monologue (sometimes introduced by another speaker) giving information on an everyday topic, e.g. a radio programme or talk from a guide	completing sentences	page 68
			completing a flow-chart	page 17
3	10	a conversation between two, three or four speakers in an educational or training context	labelling a map	page 64
			labelling a diagram	page 17
4	10	a monologue in an academic setting, e.g. a lecture or presentation	matching	pages 14, 66
			multiple choice	pages 14, 63, 65

Paper 2 Academic Reading 1 hour

- This paper is only taken in the Academic Module. There is a different paper for candidates taking the General Training Module (see Cambridge ESOL website). Both papers follow the same format but the kinds of texts on the two modules differ in terms of topic, genre, complexity of language and style.

- There are approximately 2,750 words in total in the three passages.

Passage	No. of questions	Text types	Task types *Each section has one or more of these tasks.*	Task information
1	13 (two or three tasks)	Texts may be from books, journals, magazines, newspapers or websites. They are suitable for reading by undergraduate or postgraduate students but are of general interest, not only for subject specialists.	multiple choice	pages 34, 76, 80
			matching	pages 28, 34, 73, 82
2	13 (three tasks)		choosing True/False/Not given	pages 23, 71
			choosing Yes/No/Not given	pages 34, 81
3	14 (three tasks)		locating information	page 28
			completing notes, a table, or a flow-chart	pages 23, 72
			completing a summary or sentences	pages 28, 77
			labelling a diagram	page 23

Paper 3 Academic Writing 1 hour

This paper is only taken in the Academic Module. There is a different paper for candidates taking the General Training Module (see Cambridge ESOL website).

Task	Suggested time and marks	Task text type and no. of words	Task information
1	20 minutes one-third of the marks for the paper	a summary of information given in a graph, chart, table or diagram 150 words minimum	pages 40, 87
2	40 minutes two-thirds of the marks for the paper	a discussion essay in response to a statement of opinion or ideas 250 words minimum	pages 48, 90

Paper 4 Speaking 11–14 minutes

This paper is common to both the Academic and General Training Modules.

It is a face-to-face interview with an examiner and it is recorded.

Part	Time	Task type	Task information
1	4–5 minutes	giving personal information and discussing everyday subjects	pages 55, 91
2	1 minute preparation 2 minutes talk	giving a prepared talk on a subject given by the examiner and answering one or two follow-up questions	pages 57, 92
3	4–5 minutes	a discussion with the examiner arising from the topic of Part 2, offering the opportunity to discuss more abstract issues and ideas	pages 59, 94

Further information

The information about IELTS contained in *IELTS Trainer* is designed to be an overview of the exam. For a full description of IELTS, including information about task types, testing focus and preparation for the exam, please see the *IELTS Handbook*, which can be obtained from Cambridge ESOL at the address below or from the website at: www.CambridgeESOL.org.

University of Cambridge ESOL Examinations

1 Hills Road

Cambridge CB1 2EU

United Kingdom

What is Listening Section 1?

- a conversation between two people, either face to face or on the phone
- the subject is a topic of general interest (e.g. booking a holiday or course of study)
- one or two tasks (e.g. note completion)
- an example and 10 questions

What does it test?

- understanding specific information (e.g. dates, everyday objects, places, etc.)
- spelling

Useful language: spelling

If you are asked to write the name of a street, person, company, etc., it will be spelt for you. You need to be very familiar with the names of the letters of the alphabet as you only hear them once.

 1 Listen and repeat the names of these letters.

     A   E   I   S

2 Now listen to these letters and put them in the correct column according to how we pronounce their names.

     C F G H J K L N O R T U V W X Y

Four of the letters don't fit in any of the columns. Which are they?

A	E	I	S
	C		

 3 Listen to some words being spelt out and write down what you hear. Read the word you have written. Can you say it? If not, maybe you missed a vowel!

1 Address: 23 .... Road
2 Name of company: .... Limited
3 Name: Anna ....
4 Meeting place: .... School
5 Name of village: ....
6 Website address: www. .... .com

Task information: *Note completion*

This task requires you to fill the gaps in the notes someone makes during a conversation. The notes are in the same order as the information you hear. There are other similar completion tasks that you will see: tables (e.g. Test 1 Section 4), sentences (e.g. Test 3 Section 4) and forms (e.g. Test 2 Section 1).

You have to:

- listen to a conversation – you hear it once only.
- write one/two/three words or a number or date in each gap in the notes.
- write the exact words you hear.
- spell everything correctly.
- transfer your answers to the answer sheet after all four listening sections.

Tip! When a letter is repeated, we say 'double', e.g. EE is 'double E'.

Useful language: numbers

🎧 **05** Listen to these sentences and write the number you hear in the gaps.

1 .... King Street
2 Family ticket costs $ ....
3 Mobile phone number: ....
4 Theatre opened in ....
5 Secretary is in Room ....
6 Cost of flight: £ ....

Tip! The numbers you write in the exam will be a year, a price, a phone number or part of an address, etc.

Advice

3 When we say a phone number, we can pronounce 0 as 'oh', or say 'zero'.

6 When we talk about money we say, for example 'four pound(s)/dollar(s)/euro(s) fifty' (£4.50 / $4.50 / €4.50).

Useful language: dates

🎧 **06** Listen to these sentences and write the dates you hear in the gaps.

1 The course begins on ....
2 Date of birth: ....
3 Date of appointment: ....
4 The wedding will take place on ....
5 Date of arrival in New York: ....
6 Date of interview: ....

Advice

2 We say dates like 1985 or 2014 as 'nineteen eighty-five' and 'twenty fourteen'. For years between 2000 and 2010, we can say, for example, 'two thousand and one'.

Tip! You can write a date in different ways to get a mark (e.g. 3rd March, March 3 or 3 March). This fits the 'one word and/or a number' in the instruction.

Useful language: measurements

🎧 **07** Listen to these sentences and write the measurement you hear in the gaps.

1 Mount Everest is .... high.
2 Distance from Wellington to Auckland: ....
3 John's height: ....
4 Add .... flour to sugar.
5 Weight: ....
6 Width of desk: ....

Tip! You can write the whole measurement or an abbreviation (e.g. 25 metres or 25m, 19 kilometres/kilometers or 19km).

Useful language: deciding what to write in the gaps

Look at the sample exam task below and complete this table.

Tip! Predicting what type of word will go into each gap helps you to be ready to hear it during the recording.

Which gaps need ...		What tells you this?
a date?	1	
a distance?		
only numbers?		
a price?		
a website address?		
nouns:		
• a meal or kind of food?		
• a place?		
• a facility?		
• clothes or a piece of equipment?		
• an event?		

Pony-trekking holiday

Example	Answer
Holiday lasts	........8........ days.

Holiday starts on **1** ....

Children must be over **2** .... years.

Group rides **3** .... each day on average.

Hats provided but not **4** ....

Holiday costs **5** £.................... per person

All food included except **6** ....

Camp site has a **7** ....

Find more information at www. **8** .... .com

At least one day is spent riding in the **9** ....

A **10** .... will take place one evening.

Action plan for *Note completion*

1 Look at the instructions to find out how many words you can write.

2 Look at the heading and read through the notes. There is time to do this before you listen.

3 Look at the gaps and think about what kinds of word or number are needed (e.g. a date, a distance, an address, a noun).

4 Listen to the introduction, which tells you what the recording is about.

5 Listen carefully to the conversation and focus on each question in turn. As soon as you've written the answer to one question, listen for the answer to the next.

Tip! Write an answer in every gap even if you aren't sure about it. A guess might get a mark but an empty space can't!

 08 *Questions 1–10*

Complete the notes below.

*Write no more than **TWO WORDS AND/OR A NUMBER** for each answer.*

Tip! Remember you only hear the recording once.

Tip! If one of your answers is more than two words and a number, it is wrong!

Cycling holiday in Austria

Example	Answer
Most suitable holiday lasts	........10........ days.

Holiday begins on **1** ....

No more than **2** .... people in cycling group.

Each day, group cycles **3** .... on average.

Some of the hotels have a **4** ....

Holiday costs **5** £ .... per person without flights.

All food included except **6** ....

Essential to bring a **7** ....

Discount possible on equipment at www. **8** .... .com

Possible that the **9** .... may change.

Guided tour of a **10** .... is arranged.

Advice

The words you hear are usually different from the words in the notes, except for the word(s) you have to write.

1 Make sure you write the whole date.

2 What question does the woman ask which tells you the answer is coming? Which words in the man's answer mean 'no more than'?

3 Which word tells you the answer is coming? Which words do you hear that mean 'on average'?

6 If the word you hear is plural, don't forget to write the 's'.

7 Which words do you hear which tell you that you will soon hear the answer?

8 Write only the missing word(s). There's no need to write www. and .com on the answer sheet.

10 You must spell everything correctly but both American and British English spelling are acceptable here. Check your spelling when you transfer your answers.

What is Listening Section 2?

- a talk / speech / announcement / recorded message / radio excerpt given by one person, sometimes with an introduction by another person
- the subject is a topic of general interest (e.g. what's on, a place of interest)
- usually two tasks (e.g. multiple choice, matching, completing a flow-chart)
- ten questions – there is a brief pause in the recording before the start of the next task

What does it test?

- understanding specific factual information
- selecting relevant information from what you hear

Task information: *Multiple choice (three options)*

Multiple-choice questions usually focus on the details. They follow the order of the recording.

You have to:

- listen to the recording – you hear it ONCE only.
- choose from options A, B or C to answer a question or complete a statement so that it means the same as the recording.
- transfer your answers to the answer sheet after all four listening sections.

There is another kind of multiple-choice task – see Test 2 Listening Section 2.

Task information: *Matching information*

Matching information requires you to listen to detailed information and relate it to a number of places, people, etc.

You have to:

- listen to part of the recording – you hear it ONCE only.
- match one piece of information from the box to each question.
- transfer your answers to the answer sheet after all four listening sections.

There are other kinds of matching task (e.g. Test 2 Listening Section 3, Test 4 Listening Section 3).

Useful language: paraphrasing

In many IELTS tasks, you have to choose a correct answer from a number of options. The options express ideas using different words from the recording.

Match these phrases (1–10) to ones with similar meanings (a–j).

1 a wide variety
2 recently
3 easy to get to
4 no more than
5 a peaceful spot
6 birthday
7 has a view of
8 is different
9 upmarket
10 saucepans

a a convenient location
b a special occasion
c not long ago
d looks out over
e a huge range
f has changed
g the maximum number
h kitchen equipment
i a quiet place
j luxury

Action plan for *Multiple choice (three options)*

1 Read the questions. They give you an idea of what the recording will be about and what information you should listen for.

2 Listen to the introduction. It tells you what the recording is about.

3 Follow the recording by listening for the answer to each question.

Tip! Listen out for key words, so that you know which question to answer.

4 As soon as you've chosen the answer to a question, listen for the answer to the next one.

5 Check your answers and then transfer them to the answer sheet at the end of the Listening test.

09 *Questions 11–14*

*Choose the correct letter, **A, B** or **C**.*

11 The market is now situated

    A   under a car park.
    B   beside the cathedral.
    C   near the river.

12 On only one day a week the market sells

    A   antique furniture.
    B   local produce.
    C   hand-made items.

13 The area is well known for

    A   ice cream.
    B   a cake.
    C   a fish dish.

14 What change has taken place in the harbour area?

    A   Fish can now be bought from the fishermen.
    B   The restaurants have moved to a different part.
    C   There are fewer restaurants than there used to be.

Advice

11 The prepositions on the recording are different from the ones here. Check that the answer you choose means the same as what you hear.

12 Think about the kinds of word you might hear before you listen (e.g. what is 'local produce'?).

13 Although the questions follow the order of the recording, each set of options (A, B, C) may not.

14 Read the question carefully. You need to listen for what has **changed**.

Action plan for *Matching information*

1 Read the options in the box. Think about words you might hear that have a similar meaning.

Tip! At the end of the first task there is a pause. Use this time to read the questions for the next task.

2 Listen to the instructions for the task (if this is the first task).

3 Look at the names of places, people or things that you need to match to the options.

4 Look at the options in the box while you listen to the recording. Choose one answer to each question.

Tip! If you can't choose between two answers for one question, write them both down for now. One might be the answer to a later question, then you will know you can't choose it twice.

5 Check your answers and then transfer them to the answer sheet at the end of the Listening test. Make sure you transfer the answers for both tasks!

 09 *Questions 15–20*

Which advantage is mentioned for each of the following restaurants?

*Choose **SIX** answers from the box and write the correct letter, **A–H**, next to questions 15–20.*

```
┌─────────────────────────────────────────┐
│              Advantages                  │
│   A    the decoration                    │
│   B    easy parking                      │
│   C    entertainment                     │
│   D    excellent service                 │
│   E    good value                        │
│   F    good views                        │
│   G    quiet location                    │
│   H    wide menu                         │
└─────────────────────────────────────────┘
```

15 Merrivales   ....

16 The Lobster Pot   ....

17 Elliots   ....

18 The Cabin   ....

19 The Olive Tree   ....

20 The Old School Restaurant   ....

Tip! You can only choose each option (Advantages A–H) once, so two of the options aren't needed.

Tip! The options are in alphabetical order, not in the order you hear them.

Advice

B For some restaurants you will hear information about parking but it might not be 'easy'.

D You will hear information about service but it might not be 'excellent'. The answer is only correct if the meaning matches exactly what you hear.

Tip! The restaurants (15–20) are in the order you hear them so listen for each one in turn.

What is Listening Section 3?

- a discussion between two to four speakers (e.g. between one or more students and/or a university teacher)
- the subject is some aspect of academic life (e.g. a past or future project)
- up to three tasks (e.g. flow-chart, multiple choice, labelling a diagram)
- 10 questions – there is a brief pause in the discussion between the parts that relate to each of the tasks

What does it test?

- identifying key facts and ideas and how they relate to each other
- identifying speakers' attitudes and opinions

Task information: *Flow-chart completion*

Flow-chart completion requires you to follow the development of a discussion. The steps in the flow-chart are in the same order as what you hear.

You have to:

- listen to part of the discussion – you hear it **once** only.
- choose one option (**A**, **B**, **C**, etc.) from the box to complete each space in the flow-chart according to what you hear.
- transfer your answers to the answer sheet after all four listening sections.

There is another kind of *flow-chart completion* task – see Test 5 Listening Section 4.

Task information: *Diagram labelling*

Diagram labelling requires you to transfer the information you hear to a simple picture or plan. You need to follow language expressing where things are.

You have to:

- listen to part of the discussion – you hear it **once** only.
- choose the correct words from a list to label the diagram.
- write **A**, **B**, **C**, etc. in the spaces on the diagram. There are always more words in the box than you need.
- transfer your answers to the answer sheet after all four listening sections.

There are other kinds of *diagram-labelling* task (e.g. Test 2 Listening Section 2, Test 5 Listening Section 3).

Action plan for *Flow-chart completion*

1 Read the instructions and check how many gaps there are in the flow-chart.

2 Look at the heading of the flow-chart to find out the topic of the discussion.

3 Look at the flow-chart and try to predict what the discussion will be about.

4 Read the list of options in the box.

Tip! Look at each line of the flow-chart in turn. Think about which of the words in the box might fit each space.

5 Listen carefully to the conversation, using the flow-chart to help you follow it.

Tip! The words you hear before the missing word may be synonyms of the words in the flow-chart.

6 Transfer your answers to the answer sheet at the end of the Listening test. Make sure you transfer the answers for both tasks!

Questions 21–26

Complete the flow-chart below.

Choose **SIX** answers from the box and write the correct letter, **A–I**, next to questions 21–26.

A	actors
B	furniture
C	background noise
D	costumes
E	local council
F	equipment
G	shooting schedule
H	understudies
I	shopowners

Tip! Look at the list in the box and the flow-chart before you begin.

Advice

A–I These items may be mentioned in any order.

Three of them will not be needed.

Tip! Focus on each question in turn. As soon as you have answered one question, look at the next line.

FILM PROJECT

visit locations and discuss **21**............

contact the **22**............ about roadworks

plan the **23**............

hold auditions and recheck availability of the **24**............

choose the **25**............ from the volunteers

rehearse

collect **26**............ and organise food and transport

Advice

21 The answer must be something they plan to talk about when they go somewhere.

22 Probably a person or organisation.

24 The answer comes after they have talked about auditions. Listen out for words which mean 'recheck' and 'availability'.

25 This answer is likely to be A, H or I because they are people.

26 The answer will come after they have talked about rehearsals.

Tip! As soon as the first part ends, look at the next task.

Action plan for *Diagram labelling*

1 Look at the instructions and check how many parts of the diagram you have to label.

2 Look at the heading of the diagram to find out the topic of the discussion.

3 Look at the diagram and read the labels.

Tip! You hear the information you need in the same order as the numbering of the diagram.

4 Read the list in the box. Think about what you might hear.

Tip! There are always more items in the box than you need.

5 Transfer your answers to the answer sheet at the end of the test. Make sure you transfer the answers for both tasks!

🎧 10 Questions 27–30

Choose four answers from the box and write the correct letter,
***A–G**, next to questions 27–30.*

Tip! The words in the list may be mentioned in any order.

Tip! Three of these items will not be needed. They may refer to things which are not in the diagram, or things which you do not have to label.

A	lights
B	fixed camera
C	mirror
D	torches
E	wooden screen
F	bike
G	large box

Old water-mill

Advice

27 Where is the first object you have to label – inside or outside the mill?

28 This is near a labelled object. What is the object?

What is Listening Section 4?

- a lecture, talk or presentation, usually in front of an audience
- the subject is a topic of academic interest (e.g. a scientific or historical subject)
- up to three tasks (e.g. completing notes, a table or flow-chart)
- 10 questions

What does it test?

- understanding and distinguishing between ideas: reasons, causes, effects, consequences, etc.
- following the way the ideas are organised (e.g. main ideas, specific information, attitude) and the speaker's opinion
- accurate spelling

Task information: *Table completion*

Table completion requires you to follow a talk, step by step, and complete a table which gives a record of the information and ideas that you hear.

You have to:

- listen to a lecture or talk – you hear it once only.
- write one, two or three words in each gap in the table.
- write the exact words you hear. Remember to write only the missing word(s).
- spell your answers correctly on the answer sheet.
- transfer your answers to the answer sheet after all four listening sections.

Useful language: following the speaker

When completing a table (or notes, flow-chart, etc.), it is important to listen for verbal signals that show when the speaker is moving from one aspect of the topic to another. This helps you to be in the right place for each answer.

Here are four kinds of verbal signal you can listen for:

A Introducing a new aspect of the topic
B Developing the topic further
C Introducing an example
D Referring back

Read these expressions and mark each one A, B, C or D to show what kind of verbal signal it could be. For some expressions, you can use more than one letter.

1 The reason for this was ...
2 Now I want to explain a little about ...
3 Among these well-established trades, one was ...
4 Next there's the problem of ...
5 Another experiment demonstrates ...
6 I've been asked to talk to you about ...
7 It's important to recognise ...
8 Now I'd like to talk about ...
9 Anyway, for all these reasons ...
10 And another thing was ...
11 So I want to start by ...
12 Before I talk to you in detail about ...
13 I'm going to describe for you ...
14 The first one concerns ...
15 Another way of doing this was ...
16 Another interesting result ...
17 So, we've looked briefly at ...
18 Lastly, but this is really important ...
19 Another variation is ...
20 I'll now tell you how ...

Action plan for *Table completion*

1 Look at the instructions and check how many words you must write in each gap.

2 Look at the heading of the table which tells you what the recording is about.

3 Read the column headings.

4 Look at each row of the table in turn and think about the kind of word(s) you need to complete it.

Tip! The question numbers run horizontally across each row.

5 Listen and complete each gap.

6 Move on to the next row each time the speaker talks about something new.

Tip! Keep up with the speaker. If you miss an answer, forget it and move on to the next. Fill any gaps at the end with a guess.

7 Transfer your answers to the answer sheet at the end of the test.

 Questions 31–40

Complete the table below.

Write **NO MORE THAN TWO WORDS** for each answer.

Tip! The answers are words which are not in the table.

Tip! You will hear the exact word you need to write, but its context may be worded differently from the table.

EXOTIC PESTS			
Origin	**Name**	**New habitat**	**Notes**
Australia	red-backed spider	New Zealand and Japan	even on island in middle of **31** ....
England	rabbit	Australia	800 years ago: imported into England to be used for **32** ....
America	fire ants	**33** .... in Brisbane	imported by chance
Australia	**34**	Scotland	deliberately introduced in order to improve **35** .... (not effective)
New Zealand	flatworm	**36** .... Europe	accidental introduction inside imported **37** ....
Japan	**38**	Australian coastal waters	some advantages
Australia	budgerigar	urban areas of south-east **39**	smaller flocks because of arrival of **40** .... in recent years

Tip! Focus on each row in turn as you listen.

Advice

31 You know the answer is coming when you hear about New Zealand and Japan.

32 Listen for information about 800 years ago.

33 You know the answer is coming when you hear this place or these animals.

38 The extra information between answers is sometimes quite long, sometimes quite short.

What is Reading Passage 1?

- a text of up to 900 words, usually factual or descriptive
- two or three tasks, with a total of 13 questions (e.g. True/False/Not given, short-answer questions, diagram labelling)
- usually slightly easier than Passages 2 and 3

What does it test?

- understanding texts which could be included in an academic course
- the ability to follow an argument and opinions
- a range of reading skills including reading for main ideas and detail as well as understanding the structure of a text at sentence and paragraph level

Task information: *True/False/Not given*

True/False/Not given requires you to compare the information given in a series of statements with information given in the text and decide if they are the same.

You have to:

- read statements which are in the same order as the information in the text.
- scan the text to find the information you need.
- decide if the idea given in each statement agrees with the text (True), or contradicts the text (False), or if there is no information about it in the text (Not given).

Task information: *Diagram labelling*

Diagram labelling requires you to understand a detailed description, and relate it to information in a diagram. This task is often found where the text is concerned with a process or a description of something.

You have to:

- scan the text to find specific information.
- find one, two or three words or a number in the text which complete each sentence or notes and copy them into the gaps. If you spell the word(s) wrongly, you will lose marks.

Task information: *Flow-chart completion*

Flow-chart completion requires you to understand a description of a process or sequence of events.
You have to:

- scan the text to find specific information, using the words in the flow-chart to help you locate the parts you need. This may be one or more parts of the text or the whole text. The information is not always in the same order as the flow-chart.
- find one, two or three words or a number in the text which answer each question and copy them into the gaps.

There is another kind of completion task – see Test 2 Reading Passage 2.

NOW FOLLOW THE ACTION PLANS ON PAGES 25–27

You should spend about 20 minutes on **Questions 1–13**, which are based on Reading Passage 1 below.

Walking with dinosaurs

Peter L. Falkingham and his colleagues at Manchester University are developing techniques which look set to revolutionise our understanding of how dinosaurs and other extinct animals behaved.

The media image of palaeontologists who study prehistoric life is often of field workers camped in the desert in the hot sun, carefully picking away at the rock surrounding a large dinosaur bone. But Peter Falkingham has done little of that for a while now. Instead, he devotes himself to his computer. Not because he has become inundated with paperwork, but because he is a new kind of palaeontologist: a computational palaeontologist.

What few people may consider is that uncovering a skeleton, or discovering a new species, is where the research begins, not where it ends. What we really want to understand is how the extinct animals and plants behaved in their natural habitats. Drs Bill Sellers and Phil Manning from the University of Manchester use a 'genetic algorithm' – a kind of computer code that can change itself and 'evolve' – to explore how extinct animals like dinosaurs, and our own early ancestors, walked and stalked.

The fossilised bones of a complete dinosaur skeleton can tell scientists a lot about the animal, but they do not make up the complete picture and the computer can try to fill the gap. The computer model is given a digitised skeleton, and the locations of known muscles. The model then randomly activates the muscles. This, perhaps unsurprisingly, results almost without fail in the animal falling on its face. So the computer alters the activation pattern and tries again ... usually to similar effect. The modelled 'dinosaurs' quickly 'evolve'. If there is any improvement, the computer discards the old pattern and adopts the new one as the base for alteration. Eventually, the muscle activation pattern evolves a stable way of moving, the best possible solution is reached, and the dinosaur can walk, run, chase or graze. Assuming natural selection evolves the best possible solution too, the modelled animal should be moving in a manner similar to its now-extinct counterpart. And indeed, using the same method for living animals (humans, emu and ostriches) similar top speeds were achieved on the computer as in reality. By comparing their cyberspace results with real measurements of living species, the Manchester team of palaeontologists can be confident in the results computed showing how extinct prehistoric animals such as dinosaurs moved.

The Manchester University team have used the computer simulations to produce a model of a giant meat-eating dinosaur. It is called an acrocanthosaurus which literally means 'high spined lizard' because of the spines which run along its backbone. It is not really known why they are there but scientists have speculated they could have supported a hump that stored fat and water reserves. There are also those who believe that the spines acted as a support for a sail. Of these, one half think it was used as a display and could be flushed with blood and the other half think it was used as a temperature-regulating device. It may have been a mixture of the two. The skull seems out of proportion with its thick, heavy body because it is so narrow and the jaws are delicate and fine. The feet are also worthy of note as they look surprisingly small in contrast to the animal as a whole. It has a deep broad tail and powerful leg muscles to aid locomotion. It walked on its back legs and its front legs were much shorter with powerful claws.

Falkingham himself is investigating fossilised tracks, or footprints, using computer simulations to help analyse how extinct animals moved. Modern-day trackers who study the habitats of wild animals can tell you what animal made a track, whether that animal was walking or running, sometimes even the sex of the animal. But a fossil track poses a more considerable challenge to interpret in the same way. A crucial consideration is knowing what the environment including the mud, or sediment, upon which the animal walked was like millions of years ago when the track was made. Experiments can answer these questions but the number of variables is staggering. To physically recreate each scenario with a box of mud is extremely time-consuming and difficult to repeat accurately. This is where computer simulation comes in.

Falkingham uses computational techniques to model a volume of mud and control the moisture content, consistency, and other conditions to simulate the mud of prehistoric times. A footprint is then made in the digital mud by a virtual foot. This footprint can be chopped up and viewed from any angle and stress values can be extracted and calculated from inside it. By running hundreds of these simulations simultaneously on supercomputers, Falkingham can start to understand what types of footprint would be expected if an animal moved in a certain way over a given kind of ground. Looking at the variation in the virtual tracks, researchers can make sense of fossil tracks with greater confidence.

The application of computational techniques in palaeontology is becoming more prevalent every year. As computer power continues to increase, the range of problems that can be tackled and questions that can be answered will only expand.

Action plan for *True/False/Not given*

1 Look at the title and information below it and decide who or what the text is about.

2 Read the text very quickly to get an idea of what it is about. Don't worry about words you don't understand.

3 Look at the questions and underline the important words.

4 Find the paragraph which mentions the information in the first question. Read that paragraph carefully and decide if the answer is True, False or Not given.

5 Now do the same for the other questions.

 Tip! The information you need for each question is not evenly spaced through the text. Some may be close together and some further apart. There may be some paragraphs which do not relate to any of the questions.

Questions 1–6

Do the following statements agree with the information given in Reading Passage 1?

In boxes 1–6 on your answer sheet, write

TRUE	*if the statement agrees with the information*
FALSE	*if the statement contradicts the information*
NOT GIVEN	*if there is no information on this*

Tip! You will always be able to find the answer by reading the text. You never need to use your own general knowledge.

Tip! Two questions following each other may have the same answer. There is always at least one True, one False and one Not given answer.

1 In his study of prehistoric life, Peter Falkingham rarely spends time on outdoor research these days.

2 Several attempts are usually needed before the computer model of a dinosaur used by Sellers and Manning manages to stay upright.

3 When the Sellers and Manning computer model was used for people, it showed them moving faster than they are physically able to.

4 Some palaeontologists have expressed reservations about the conclusions reached by the Manchester team concerning the movement of dinosaurs.

5 An experienced tracker can analyse fossil footprints as easily as those made by live animals.

6 Research carried out into the composition of prehistoric mud has been found to be inaccurate.

Advice

1 The answer is in the first paragraph. Sometimes the first question is about information in a later paragraph and the first few paragraphs don't have a True/False/Not given question.

2 Which paragraph do you need to read? Which words tell you? You need to read several sentences to find the answer.

4 Which sentence talks about the conclusions made by the Manchester team about the movement of dinosaurs? What does it say about the opinions of other palaeontologists?

Action plan for *Diagram labelling*

If a diagram is the first task for a text, read the text through very quickly before you follow this plan so that you have a general idea of the text's structure and argument.

1 Look at the instructions and see how many words you must write.

2 Look at the heading to the diagram. This will help you find the information you need in the text.

3 Read the questions, underline the important words and decide what kind of word(s) you need for the answer (e.g. noun, verb, adjective).

4 Find the part of the text which you need and read it carefully.

Tip! The answers are usually in one or two paragraphs but they may be in a different order in the text from the questions.

5 For each question, underline the word(s) in the text which fit(s) the gap and copy it/them.

Tip! You will always be able to find the exact word(s) you need in the text.

6 Read the labels again to make sure they make sense.

Questions 7–9

Label the diagram below.

Choose **NO MORE THAN ONE WORD** *from the passage for each answer.*

Write your answers in boxes 7–9 on your answer sheet.

Tip! Sometimes you only need to write one word, sometimes two or three. Read the instructions carefully.

Tip! Which paragraph(s) talk(s) about a model of an acrocanthosaurus?

A model of an acrocanthosaurus

Dinosaur's name comes from spines. One theory: they were necessary to hold up a **7** .... which helped control body heat.

Skull is **8** .... compared with rest of body.

9 .... made easier by wide tail and highly developed muscles in legs.

Advice

7 There are several theories about the spines. Which one talks about 'body heat'? Which words are used?

8 What kind of word do you need to look for?

9 Find the sentences which talk about the tail and legs. Which word means the same as 'made easier'?

Action plan for *Flow-chart completion*

If a flow-chart is the first task for a text, read the text through very quickly before you follow this plan so that you have a general idea of the text's structure and argument.

1 Look at the instructions and see how many words you must write.

2 Read the heading to the flow-chart. This will help you find the part(s) of the text you need.

3 Read the flow-chart. Underline the important words in each question and decide what kind of word(s) you need (e.g. noun, verb, adjective).

4 Find the part(s) of the text you need and read it carefully.

5 For each question, underline the word(s) in the text which fit(s) the gap and copy it/them.

Tip! You never need to change the word you copy (e.g. from a noun into a verb, or from singular to plural).

6 Read the sentences again to make sure they make sense.

Questions 10–13

Complete the flow-chart below.

Write **NO MORE THAN TWO WORDS** *for each answer.*

Peter Falkingham's computer model

Mud is simulated with attention to its texture and thickness and how much **10** .... it contains.

⬇

A virtual foot produces a footprint in the mud.

⬇

The footprint is dissected and examined from all angles.

⬇

Levels of **11** .... are measured within the footprint.

⬇

Multiple simulations relate footprints to different types of **12** ....

⬇

More accurate interpretation of **13** .... is possible.

Tip! Check the instructions and make sure you write the correct number of words.

Tip! Some parts of the flow-chart don't have a gap in them. They help you to find the right part of the text.

Advice

10 *Copy the word carefully. Don't make a spelling mistake.*

13 *You need two words for this answer.*

What is Reading Passage 2?

- a text of up to 900 words
- two or three different tasks, with a total of 13 or 14 questions

Task information: *Locating information*

Locating information requires you to scan a text to find specific information in a paragraph.

You have to:

- read a text divided into labelled paragraphs.
- read statements which focus on details in a paragraph.
- find which paragraph contains the information in each question. The answer may be in one sentence or phrase in a paragraph, or you may need to read more than one sentence.

Task information: *Matching names*

Matching names requires you to relate information, ideas or opinions in the text to a number of people, places, dates, etc.

You have to:

- read a list of statements and match them to a list of options by finding the information in the text. You may have to match people, cities, projects, businesses, schools, theories, plants or dates with events, techniques, discoveries, facilities, etc.
- for each question, write the letter of the statement which matches it. DON'T put the letter of the paragraph where you find the answer.

There are other kinds of matching task – see Test 2 Reading Passage 2.

Task information: *Summary completion*

Summary completion requires you to understand the main points of part of the text.

You have to:

- read the summary and identify the part(s) of the text to which it refers. The information may not be in the same order as in the text.
- complete the gaps in the summary by choosing a word or words from the text.

There is another kind of summary task (e.g. Test 4 Reading Passage 3).

NOW FOLLOW THE ACTION PLANS ON PAGES 31–33

*You should spend about 20 minutes on **Questions 14–26**, which are based on Reading Passage 2 below.*

The robots are coming – or are they?

What is the current state of play in Artificial Intelligence?

A Can robots advance so far that they become the ultimate threat to our existence? Some scientists say no, and dismiss the very idea of Artificial Intelligence. The human brain, they argue, is the most complicated system ever created, and any machine designed to reproduce human thought is bound to fail. Physicist Roger Penrose of Oxford University and others believe that machines are physically incapable of human thought. Colin McGinn of Rutgers University backs this up when he says that Artificial Intelligence 'is like sheep trying to do complicated psychoanalysis. They just don't have the conceptual equipment they need in their limited brains'.

B Artificial Intelligence, or AI, is different from most technologies in that scientists still understand very little about how intelligence works. Physicists have a good understanding of Newtonian mechanics and the quantum theory of atoms and molecules, whereas the basic laws of intelligence remain a mystery. But a sizeable number of mathematicians and computer scientists, who are specialists in the area, are optimistic about the possibilities. To them it is only a matter of time before a thinking machine walks out of the laboratory. Over the years, various problems have impeded all efforts to create robots. To attack these difficulties, researchers tried to use the 'top-down approach', using a computer in an attempt to program all the essential rules onto a single disc. By inserting this into a machine, it would then become self-aware and attain human-like intelligence.

C In the 1950s and 1960s great progress was made, but the shortcomings of these prototype robots soon became clear. They were huge and took hours to navigate across a room. Meanwhile, a fruit fly, with a brain containing only a fraction of the computing power, can effortlessly navigate in three dimensions. Our brains, like the fruit fly's, unconsciously recognise what we see by performing countless calculations. This unconscious awareness of patterns is exactly what computers are missing. The second problem is robots' lack of common sense. Humans know that water is wet and that mothers are older than their daughters. But there is no mathematics that can express these truths. Children learn the intuitive laws of biology and physics by interacting with the real world. Robots know only what has been programmed into them.

D Because of the limitations of the top-down approach to Artificial Intelligence, attempts have been made to use a 'bottom-up' approach instead – that is, to try to imitate evolution and the way a baby learns. Rodney Brooks was the director of MIT's Artificial Intelligence laboratory, famous for its lumbering 'top-down' walking robots. He changed the course of research when he explored the unorthodox idea of tiny 'insectoid' robots that learned to walk by bumping into things instead of computing mathematically the precise position of their feet. Today many of the descendants of Brooks' insectoid robots are on Mars gathering data for NASA (The National Aeronautics and Space Administration), running across the dusty landscape of the planet. For all their successes in mimicking the behaviour of insects, however, robots using neural networks have performed miserably when their programmers have tried to duplicate in them the behaviour of higher organisms such as mammals. MIT's Marvin Minsky summarises the problems of AI: 'The history of AI is sort of funny because the first real accomplishments were beautiful things, like a machine that could do well in a maths course. But then we started to try to make machines that could answer questions about simple children's stories. There's no machine today that can do that.'

E There are people who believe that eventually there will be a combination between the top-down and bottom-up, which may provide the key to Artificial Intelligence. As adults, we blend the two approaches. It has been suggested that our emotions represent the quality that most distinguishes us as human, that it is impossible for machines ever to have emotions. Computer expert Hans Moravec thinks that in the future robots will be programmed with emotions such as fear to protect themselves so that they can signal to humans when their batteries are running low, for example. Emotions are vital in decision-making. People who have suffered a certain kind of brain injury lose the ability to experience emotions and become unable to make decisions. Without emotions to guide them, they debate endlessly over their options. Moravec points out that as robots become more intelligent and are able to make choices, they could likewise become paralysed with indecision. To aid them, robots of the future might need to have emotions hardwired into their brains.

F There is no universal consensus as to whether machines can be conscious, or even, in human terms, what consciousness means. Minsky suggests the thinking process in our brain is not localised but spread out, with different centres competing with one another at any given time. Consciousness may then be viewed as a sequence of thoughts and images issuing from these different, smaller 'minds', each one competing for our attention. Robots might eventually attain a 'silicon consciousness'. Robots, in fact, might one day embody an architecture for thinking and processing information that is different from ours – but also indistinguishable. If that happens, the question of whether they really 'understand' becomes largely irrelevant. A robot that has perfect mastery of syntax, for all practical purposes, understands what is being said.

Action plan for *Locating information*

1 Look at the title and subtitle and decide who or what the text is about.

2 Read the questions quickly and see what else you can predict about the text.

3 Read the text very quickly to get a general idea of what it is about.

4 Read each question carefully and find the part of the text which contains the same information as the question.

Tip! Some paragraphs may contain the answers to more than one question and some paragraphs may not contain any answers.

5 Check that the paragraph you choose as the answer has exactly the same information as the question.

Questions 14–20

Reading Passage 2 has six paragraphs, *A–F*.

Which paragraph contains the following information?

Write the correct letter, A–F, in boxes 14–20 on your answer sheet.
NB You may use any letter more than once.

14 an insect that proves the superiority of natural intelligence over Artificial Intelligence

15 robots being able to benefit from their mistakes

16 many researchers not being put off believing that Artificial Intelligence will eventually be developed

17 an innovative approach that is having limited success

18 the possibility of creating Artificial Intelligence being doubted by some academics

19 no generally accepted agreement of what our brains do

20 robots not being able to extend their intelligence in the same way as humans

Advice

14 Scan the text quickly to find any paragraphs which mention insects. Read those paragraphs carefully. Which matches the information in the question? You need to find a reference to a particular insect rather than insects in general.

15 Scan the text quickly to find which paragraph talks about robots learning from their mistakes. Most of the paragraphs talk about the things robots aren't good at but only one paragraph mentions them learning from mistakes.

16 All the paragraphs mention researchers but which paragraph mentions some who are positive about the future of Artificial Intelligence? Which words in the text mean 'not being put off'?

17 Check the tense in this question. Find a paragraph in the text which mentions an innovative approach. Is it having limited success now?

18 The important word here is 'doubted'.

19 Find a phrase which means 'generally accepted agreement'. An idea in the text will probably be expressed in the question with different words.

Action plan for *Matching names*

If *Matching names* is the first task for a text, read the text through very quickly before you follow this plan so that you have a general idea of the text's structure and argument.

1 Look at the list of names. Find them in the text and underline them.

Tip! Sometimes the names are in more than one place.

2 For each name, read all the things that person says.

3 For each name, choose the statement which matches one of the things they say. Each name can be matched with only one statement.

Tip! There are two statements which don't match any of the names.

Questions 21–23

Look at the following people (Questions 21–23) and the list of statements below.

*Match each person with the correct statement, **A–E**.*

*Write the correct letter, **A–E**, in boxes 21–23 on your answer sheet.*

Tip! Write the letter of the correct statement, *not* the paragraph where you find the answer.

21 Colin McGinn

22 Marvin Minsky

23 Hans Moravec

A	Artificial Intelligence may require something equivalent to feelings in order to succeed.
B	Different kinds of people use different parts of the brain.
C	Tests involving fiction have defeated Artificial Intelligence so far.
D	People have intellectual capacities which do not exist in computers.
E	People have no reason to be frightened of robots.

Advice

In which paragraphs can you find the opinions of these people? Other people are also quoted in the text but their opinions are not important here.

21 Read what Colin McGinn says and match it to one of the statements. Why is A wrong?

22 Marvin Minsky is quoted in two different paragraphs. Read what he says in both places and match one of the statements to what he says.

23 Read what Hans Moravec says and match it to one of the statements.

Action plan for *Summary completion*

If *Summary completion* is the first task for a text, read the text through very quickly before you follow this plan so that you have a general idea of the text's structure and argument.

1 Read the instructions and check how many words you have to write.

2 Locate the part(s) of the text you need by reading the summary and underlining important words. The title of the summary may help you.

Tip! The information you need may be in one paragraph or it may be spread over a longer part of the text.

3 Look at each numbered gap and decide what kind of word(s) you need (e.g. noun, verb, adjective).

4 Read the relevant part(s) of the text and underline the word(s) which you think fit(s) in each gap.

5 Write the words in the gaps and then read the summary again. It should make sense and summarise exactly what the text says.

Tip! Write each word exactly as it appears in the text. Check if it is singular or plural.

Questions 24–26

Complete the summary below.

*Choose **ONE WORD ONLY** from the passage for each answer.*

Write your answers in boxes 24–26 on your answer sheet.

> ## When will we have a thinking machine?
>
> Despite some advances, the early robots had certain weaknesses. They were given the information they needed on a **24** .... This was known as the 'top-down' approach and enabled them to do certain tasks but they were unable to recognise **25** .... Nor did they have any intuition or ability to make decisions based on experience. Rodney Brooks tried a different approach. Robots similar to those invented by Brooks are to be found on **26** .... where they are collecting information.

Advice

Underline the important words in the summary before you start. Which part of the text will you read? Which words in the text mean 'early robots'?

Which word in the summary means 'shortcomings'? Find the part of the text which explains the 'top-down' approach and read it.

24 *Find the sentence about how robots were given information. Which word will you write?*

25 *Find the part of the text about what robots cannot recognise. Which word will you write?*

26 *Find the part of the text about Rodney Brooks.*

What is Reading Passage 3?

- a text of up to 950 words
- two or three different tasks, with a total of 13 or 14 questions (e.g. Yes/No/Not given, multiple choice and summary completion)
- usually slightly more challenging than Passages 1 and 2

Task information: *Yes/No/Not given*

Yes/No/Not given requires you to identify and understand opinions, ideas and attitudes.

You have to:

- read statements which focus on the writer's ideas as expressed in the text. The statements are in the same order as the ideas in the text.
- scan the text to find where the writer discusses the relevant topic.
- decide if the idea given in each statement agrees with opinions/ideas of the writer (Yes), or contradicts them (No), or if there is no information about that idea in the text (Not given).

Task information: *Multiple choice*

Multiple choice requires both general and detailed understanding of the text.

You have to:

- read questions or incomplete statements which focus on the ideas and information in the text. The questions are in the same order as the ideas in the text. They may refer to a small part of the text, or a long section of it. Occasionally, the last question may refer to the text as a whole.
- choose the correct option **A**, **B**, **C** or **D** to answer the question or complete the statement so that it means the same as the text. There is *never* more than one correct option.

Task information: *Matching sentence endings*

Matching sentence endings requires you to understand a number of significant ideas expressed in the text.

You have to:

- read the first halves of some sentences. These are in the same order as the information in the text so the information relating to the first half-sentence will be found in the text before the information relating to the second half-sentence, and so on.
- choose the ending for each half-sentence from a number of options **A**, **B**, **C**, etc. so that the complete sentence correctly expresses an idea or opinion in the text.

NOW FOLLOW THE ACTION PLANS ON PAGES 37–39

You should spend about 20 minutes on **Questions 27–40**, which are based on Reading Passage 3 below.

Endangered languages

'Never mind whales, save the languages',
says Peter Monaghan, graduate of the Australian National University

Worried about the loss of rainforests and the ozone layer? Well, neither of those is doing any worse than a large majority of the 6,000 to 7,000 languages that remain in use on Earth. One half of the survivors will almost certainly be gone by 2050, while 40% more will probably be well on their way out. In their place, almost all humans will speak one of a handful of megalanguages – Mandarin, English, Spanish.

Linguists know what causes languages to disappear, but less often remarked is what happens on the way to disappearance: languages' vocabularies, grammars and expressive potential all diminish as one language is replaced by another. 'Say a community goes over from speaking a traditional Aboriginal language to speaking a creole*,' says Australian Nick Evans, a leading authority on Aboriginal languages, 'you leave behind a language where there's very fine vocabulary for the landscape. All that is gone in a creole. You've just got a few words like 'gum tree' or whatever. As speakers become less able to express the wealth of knowledge that has filled ancestors' lives with meaning over millennia, it's no wonder that communities tend to become demoralised.'

If the losses are so huge, why are relatively few linguists combating the situation? Australian linguists, at least, have achieved a great deal in terms of preserving traditional languages. Australian governments began in the 1970s to support an initiative that has resulted in good documentation of most of the 130 remaining Aboriginal languages. In England, another Australian, Peter Austin, has directed one of the world's most active efforts to limit language loss, at the University of London. Austin heads a programme that has trained many documentary linguists in England as well as in language-loss hotspots such as West Africa and South America.

At linguistics meetings in the US, where the endangered-language issue has of late been something of a flavour of the month, there is growing evidence that not all approaches to the preservation of languages will be particularly helpful. Some linguists are boasting, for example, of more and more sophisticated means of capturing languages: digital recording and storage, and internet and mobile phone technologies. But these are encouraging the 'quick dash' style of recording trip: fly in, switch on digital recorder, fly home, download to hard drive, and store gathered material for future research. That's not quite what some endangered-language specialists have been seeking for more than 30 years. Most loud and untiring has been Michael Krauss, of the University of Alaska. He has often complained that linguists are playing with non-essentials while most of their raw data is disappearing.

Who is to blame? That prominent linguist Noam Chomsky, say Krauss and many others. Or, more precisely, they blame those linguists who have been obsessed with his approaches. Linguists who go out into communities to study, document and describe languages, argue that theoretical linguists, who draw conclusions about how languages work, have had so much influence that linguistics has largely ignored the continuing disappearance of languages.

Chomsky, from his post at the Massachusetts Institute of Technology, has been the great man of theoretical linguistics for far longer than he has been known as a political commentator. His landmark work of 1957 argues that all languages exhibit certain universal grammatical features, encoded in the human mind. American linguists, in particular, have focused largely on theoretical concerns ever since, even while doubts have mounted about Chomsky's universals.

* a language developed from a mixture of two different languages

Austin and Co. are in no doubt that because languages are unique, even if they do tend to have common underlying features, creating dictionaries and grammars requires prolonged and dedicated work. This requires that documentary linguists observe not only languages' structural subtleties, but also related social, historical and political factors. Such work calls for persistent funding of field scientists who may sometimes have to venture into harsh and even hazardous places. Once there, they may face difficulties such as community suspicion. As Nick Evans says, a community who speak an endangered language may have reasons to doubt or even oppose efforts to preserve it. They may have seen support and funding for such work come and go. They may have given up using the language with their children, believing they will benefit from speaking a more widely understood one.

Plenty of students continue to be drawn to the intellectual thrill of linguistics field work. That's all the more reason to clear away barriers, contend Evans, Austin and others. The highest barrier, they agree, is that the linguistics profession's emphasis on theory gradually wears down the enthusiasm of linguists who work in communities. Chomsky disagrees. He has recently begun to speak in support of language preservation. But his linguistic, as opposed to humanitarian, argument is, let's say, unsentimental: the loss of a language, he states, 'is much more of a tragedy for linguists whose interests are mostly theoretical, like me, than for linguists who focus on describing specific languages, since it means the permanent loss of the most relevant data for general theoretical work'. At the moment, few institutions award doctorates for such work, and that's the way it should be, he reasons. In linguistics, as in every other discipline, he believes that good descriptive work requires thorough theoretical understanding and should also contribute to building new theory. But that's precisely what documentation does, objects Evans. The process of immersion in a language, to extract, analyse and sum it up, deserves a PhD because it is 'the most demanding intellectual task a linguist can engage in'.

Action plan for *Yes/No/Not given*

1 Look at the title and subtitle and think about who or what the text is about.

2 Read the text very quickly. Don't worry about words you don't understand.

3 Look at the statements. Underline the important words.

4 Find the part of the text which discusses the ideas in the first statement. Read it carefully.

5 Decide whether the first statement agrees with what the writer says in the text. Choose *Yes, No* or *Not given*.

Tip! Be sure to read enough to check you have understood the writer's views properly.

6 Do the same for the other statements.

Questions 27–32

Do the following statements agree with the views of the writer in Reading Passage 3?

In boxes 27–32 on your answer sheet, write

YES	*if the statement agrees with the views of the writer*
NO	*if the statement contradicts the views of the writer*
NOT GIVEN	*if it is impossible to say what the writer thinks about this*

Tip! Remember, it is the **writer's** views you need to check, not other people's.

27 By 2050 only a small number of languages will be flourishing. *Yes*

28 Australian academics' efforts to record existing Aboriginal languages have been too limited. *No*

29 The use of technology in language research is proving unsatisfactory in some respects. *Yes.*

30 Chomsky's political views have overshadowed his academic work. *Not given*

31 Documentary linguistics studies require long-term financial support. *Yes*

32 Chomsky's attitude to disappearing languages is too emotional. *No*

Advice

27 Are the ideas in the question referred to in the first or second paragraph?

28 Which words in the statement suggest an attitude towards the work of Australian linguists? Is it critical or positive?

29 What does 'the use of technology' mean? Find this in the text. Read around the sentence where it is mentioned. Why is it mentioned?

30 Think carefully about the implications of 'overshadowed'. What does the writer say about Chomsky's political views?

Action plan for *Multiple choice*

If the *multiple-choice* questions are the first task for a text, read the text through quickly before you follow this plan so that you have a general idea of the text's structure and argument.

1 Read each question or incomplete statement and the options A–D.

2 Find the part of the text that you need and think about what the answer might be. Make sure you read far enough to cover everything relevant to the question.

3 Reread all four options carefully and choose the one you believe to be correct.

Tip! Be careful – the incorrect options may use similar words to those in the text, but they will be clearly wrong.

Questions 33–36

*Choose the correct letter, **A**, **B**, **C** or **D**.*

33 The writer mentions rainforests and the ozone layer

  A because he believes anxiety about environmental issues is unfounded.

  B to demonstrate that academics in different disciplines share the same problems.

  C because they exemplify what is wrong with the attitudes of some academics.

  D to make the point that the public should be equally concerned about languages.

34 What does Nick Evans say about speakers of a creole?

  A They lose the ability to express ideas which are part of their culture.

  B Older and younger members of the community have difficulty communicating.

  C They express their ideas more clearly and concisely than most people.

  D Accessing practical information causes problems for them.

35 What is similar about West Africa and South America, from the linguist's point of view?

  A The English language is widely used by academics and teachers.

  B The documentary linguists who work there were trained by Australians.

  C Local languages are disappearing rapidly in both places.

  D There are now only a few undocumented languages there.

36 Michael Krauss has frequently pointed out that

  A linguists are failing to record languages before they die out.

  B linguists have made poor use of improvements in technology.

  C linguistics has declined in popularity as an academic subject.

  D linguistics departments are underfunded in most universities.

Tip! Multiple-choice questions follow the order of the text.

Advice

33 Look at the first paragraph and find where the writer mentions rainforests and the ozone layer. Choose the answer which supports what we know about the writer's views.

34 Find the part of the text where Nick Evans talks about the speakers of a creole. What does he say about them? Remember to read the footnote here.

35 Find the part of the text which mentions these places. 'Hotspot' is used here as a metaphor. What do you think it implies? Which words describe these hotspots?

36 Be careful – Krauss is mentioned more than once. What do you think 'playing with non-essentials' refers to?

Action plan for *Matching sentence endings*

If *Matching sentence endings* is the first task for a text, read the text through very quickly before you follow this plan so that you have a general idea of the text's structure and argument.

1 Read the first incomplete sentence.

2 Find the part or parts of the text that you need. Make sure you read far enough to cover everything relevant to the question.

3 Read the options carefully and choose the one you believe to be correct.

> **Tip!** There are two or three options which do not match any of the first halves of sentences, but they may seem very close in meaning until you read them carefully.

4 Read each of the other incomplete sentences and repeat Steps 2 and 3 above.

> **Tip!** There may be more than one part of the text which mentions the subject of the sentence. It's important to find the right one.

Questions 37–40

*Complete each sentence with the correct ending, **A–G**, below.*

*Write the correct letter, **A–G**, in boxes 37–40 on your answer sheet.*

> **Tip!** The first halves contain clues to help you locate the correct parts of the text.

> **Tip!** These questions work in a similar way to multiple-choice questions such as Question 33, but there are more options to choose from. There is still only one correct answer for each question, however!

37 Linguists like Peter Austin believe that every language is unique *C*

38 Nick Evans suggests a community may resist attempts to save its language *A*

39 Many young researchers are interested in doing practical research *F*

40 Chomsky supports work in descriptive linguistics *B*

A	even though it is in danger of disappearing.
B	provided that it has a strong basis in theory.
C	although it may share certain universal characteristics.
D	because there is a practical advantage to it.
E	so long as the drawbacks are clearly understood.
F	in spite of the prevalence of theoretical linguistics.
G	until they realise what is involved.

> **Tip!** Read the sentence endings carefully. The linking words (*even though, provided that,* etc.) can be very important to the meaning.

What is Writing Task 1?

- a writing task based on data which is presented as a graph or bar chart, or a diagram of a process, machine or device

What does it test?

- expressing the information concisely and accurately
- use of an appropriate academic style (formal or neutral)
- accurate grammar, spelling and punctuation
- clear organisation of your ideas

Task information

This task requires you to recognise and select important and relevant points from the data.

You have to:

- summarise the data you are given in at least 150 words.
- plan, write and check your work in 20 minutes.
- write about the most important parts of the data.
- make comparisons and contrasts as appropriate.
- draw attention to relevant features of the data and interpret them.

STRATEGIES

Before you write

A Reading the question

Read the task below and think about the questions in boxes 1–5. This is the kind of task you will see in Writing Task 1.

*1 Read the **question** carefully. What does the first part of the question tell you? What **three** things does the rest of the question remind you to do?*

You should spend about 20 minutes on this task.

The bar chart below gives information about the percentage of the population living in urban areas in the whole world and in different parts of the world.

Summarise the information by selecting and reporting the main features, and make comparisons where relevant.

Write at least 150 words.

*2 Look at the **bar chart**. Give yourself time to understand it. The **title** gives you information about its purpose. What does the title of this bar chart tell you?*

*3 Look at the **key** of the bar chart. What do the three bars represent? (The **key** of a chart, graph or map explains its symbols, shading or colours.)*

Changes in percentage of population in urban areas

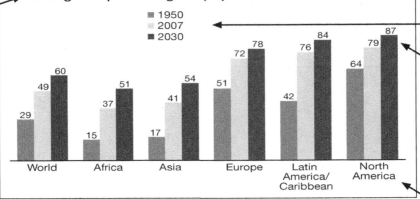

*4 Look at the **numbers** on the bar chart. What do they represent?*

*5 Look at the **labels** along the x-axis (at the bottom). What information does the bar chart contain?*

B Understanding the data

Read these sentences about the bar chart on the previous page. Which of them report the data correctly? Mark them ✔ (correct) or ✘ (incorrect).

Can you explain why the incorrect statements are wrong? Can you correct them?

1 *In North America, we can see that 64% of people already lived in cities by 1950, increasing to 79% by 2007.*

2 *This bar chart gives information about the percentage of the population living in urban areas in six regions of the world in three different years, 1950, 2007 and 2030.*

3 *According to the chart, there is a much greater change in Africa than in North America.*

4 *According to the chart, more North Americans already live in cities than in the rest of the world.*

5 *In Africa only 15% of the population lived in urban areas in the middle of the last century, but this had risen to 37% by 2007.*

6 *According to this chart, there will be twice as many Latin Americans and Caribbeans living in cities in 2030 as there were eighty years earlier.*

7 *In 2030 the percentage of the world's population living in urban areas is predicted to be just over twice what it was in 1950.*

C Selecting from the data

Look again at the task on page 40. Select which parts of the data in the bar chart are most relevant to the task. Use a highlighter pen or make notes.

Now check your answers to Exercise B and study the corrected sentences. Which sentences could you use for the following parts of your summary?

1 an opening statement of what the whole bar chart is about (find one sentence)

2 the main piece of information which you understand from the data (find one sentence)

3 a comparison or contrast, supported by data from the chart (find at least three sentences)

> **Tip!** The longest part of your summary will be comparing and contrasting. The opening sentence and main information will be **at most** two sentences each.

D Writing a summary

1 When you have analysed the data you have to interpret, and planned what you are going to write, you are ready to write your summary. Use the words in the box to fill the spaces in the sample answer below.

> compares   doubled   greatest   in spite of
> marked   shows   smaller   whereas

The bar chart **1** .... the percentage of the world's population living in urban areas in 1950 and **2** .... this with the percentage in 2007 and the projected percentage for 2030.

The proportion of the world's population living in cities will have **3** .... between 1950 and 2030. However, the change is less **4** .... in some regions than others. In North America, for example, we can see that 64% of people already lived in cities by 1950, increasing to 79% by 2007, **5** .... in Africa only 15% of the population lived in urban areas in 1950, but this rose to 37% by 2007. This represents the **6** .... change from rural to urban living, even though the percentage of Africans in cities is still **7** .... than the world average. It is also noticeable that, according to the bar chart, the proportion of the population of Latin America and the Caribbean in cities will be higher than Europe by 2030, **8** .... being lower in 1950.

2 Which is the longest part of this answer – the opening, the main idea or the comparisons and contrasts?

After you write

E Checking your answer

Read the answer at the top of page 43 as if you were checking your own work in the test. Decide whether the candidate has answered the question satisfactorily.

1 There is one spelling error. Can you find it?

2 Now correct her errors.

   a Correct 1 and 2. Find the other places where the candidate repeats these errors.

   b Fill the marked space 3 with a suitable word.

   c Correct the grammar in the other highlighted words and phrases.

   d Suggest another word to use instead of repeating 'part(s)' every time.

IELTS candidate's summary

In the chart we can see the percentage of the population who live in urban **1** area in the years 1950, 2007 and 2030. The first three columns show us the **2** result in the whole world and the other columns show the result in different parts of the world. What is very obvious from the chart is that the number of people living in urban area and also **3** .... moving to urban area is growing quite fast in all parts of the world and there **4** isn't any part that the percentage has come down. It **5** is also seen that in North America and **6** the Latin America this percentage is higher than other parts. **7** By comparing the proportion of people in cities in the rest of the world, Europe, Asia and Africa respectively have the highest percentages. The increase in the number of people in urban area is such that it is estimated that in the year 2030, approximatly 60% of the people in the world will be living in urban area.

Some of these errors are habits influenced by the writer's first language. Can you identify your own habitual errors?

Tip! Make a note of your habitual errors and check for them when you write.

Useful language: contrasting facts and ideas

We contrast facts and ideas between sentences using expressions such as *However, By contrast, On the other hand*, etc. We contrast facts and ideas within a sentence using words such as *whereas* and *while*.

1 ⊙ **What mistake has this IELTS candidate made?**

The profits of company C declined over these fifteen years. On the other hand the overall profits of company B also declined.

2 ⊙ **What mistake has this IELTS candidate made?**

The money spent by governments on research has decreased in developing countries. Whereas in industrialised countries it has doubled.

3 Without looking back at the sample answer on page 42, fill the spaces with *whereas*, or *however*, then check your answers.

The proportion of the world's population living in cities will have doubled between 1950 and 2030. **a** .... , the change is less marked in some regions than others. In North America, for example, we can see that 64% of people already lived in cities by 1950, increasing to 79% by 2007, **b** .... in Africa only 15% of the population lived in urban areas in 1950.

4 👁 Choose the correct word or phrase in *italics* in these IELTS candidates' sentences.

1 USA has the highest percentage of this group *while/however* Vietnam has the lowest.

2 In 1990, industrialised countries were spending twice as much on research compared to 1980. *Whereas/On the other hand*, expenditure in developing countries decreased during this period.

3 New Zealand has the highest percentage of women working in parliament. *By contrast/ While*, Italy has the lowest percentage of all the countries shown.

4 Going out to restaurants accounted for 15% of free time activities, *whereas/on the other hand* only about 12% of the time was used for meeting friends and socialising.

5 People aged 14–24 went to the cinema most often at this time. *However/Whereas* the percentage of people over fifty was lowest.

5 Contrast the facts and ideas in five of these pairs of sentences, using a different word or expression from the box for each one.

One pair of sentences does not offer contrasting ideas. Suggest a way of combining the two sentences to emphasise this.

| by contrast   however   on the other hand |
| whereas   while |

1 For the workforce, working conditions have always been more important than wages. Profitability has been the main concern of the management.

2 In the United States, people tend to eat early in the evening. In Spain, few people eat before nine o'clock.

3 The students at the state university showed an improved performance in the tests. Attending a private college enabled students to increase their test scores.

4 Home computers were a rarity in the 1980s. The majority of families have at least one computer now.

5 Car ownership has risen sharply in rural areas. The provision of public transport has declined.

6 A sense of humour is rated as essential by 90% of women who are looking for a partner. Only 70% of women say they want to meet someone wealthy.

6 Now use the words in the box in Exercise 5 and write some sentences about a topic you are interested in.

Useful language: expressing percentages, proportions and quantities

Try to vary the way you refer to quantities in your writing. Look at these expressions for 90% and write down ways you could refer to 10%.

90%	10%
ninety percent (of)	....
a high percentage (of)	....
nine-tenths (of)	....
nine out of ten	....
the vast majority of	....
most (of)	....
nearly all (of)	....

Useful language: talking about numbers as they get bigger and smaller

1 Match these verbs with their opposites.

1	to rise	**a**	to decrease
2	to increase	**b**	to shrink
3	to go up	**c**	to halve
4	to grow	**d**	to contract
5	to double	**e**	to fall
6	to expand	**f**	to go down

2 Which verbs from Exercise 1 can you use with these groups of words?

1 things that can be counted (e.g. number of homeowners/students, etc.)

2 things that can be described in terms of size (e.g. a company)

3 things that have monetary value (e.g. cost of living, price of houses)

3 Complete the sentences with appropriate verbs from Exercise 1 in the correct tense.

1 Audiences at the theatre ...... if another cinema opens. (–)

2 The cost of living ...... in the last forty years. (+)

3 Losing our best customer ...... our income. (÷ 2)

4 Computer use ...... sharply in the past few years. (+)

5 The company's profits ...... in 2009. (x 2)

6 Interest rates ...... if the government follows this policy. (–)

Useful language: writing about information in a chart or graph

Ⓞ **Look at the pairs of sentences written by IELTS candidates. Choose the correct one in each pair (a or b) and underline the correct phrase.**

1 **a** It can be seen that 96% of the prison population are males.
  b It is seen that 96% of the prison population are males.

2 **a** There is clear that almost 30% of men work over 45 hours a week.
  b It is clear that almost 30% of men work over 45 hours a week.

3 **a** It is easy to be seen that the number of people increased.
  b It is easy to see that the number of people increased.

4 **a** The pie chart represents the main types of employment.
  b The pie chart shows the main types of employment.

5 **a** The graphs indicate information about total government spending.
  b The graphs provide information about total government spending.

6 **a** From the charts we can find out travelling abroad is becoming more popular.
  b From the charts we can see travelling abroad is becoming more popular.

Test 1 Exam practice / Writing Task 1

In the IELTS exam, it is important not to spend more than 20 minutes on Task 1, otherwise you may not have enough time for Writing Task 2, which is longer and is worth twice as many marks.

Tip! When practising you will probably need more than 20 minutes at first. Keep a note of how long you take and try reducing the time for each practice test until you can do Task 1 in 20 minutes.

Action plan for *Bar chart* and other graphs

Before you write

This Action plan refers to a bar chart. Follow the same Action plan for other graphs and diagrams. The bar chart is similar to the one on page 40 but NOT the same.

1 Look at the task on page 47 and read the question carefully. Think about what the first part of the question tells you.

2 Look at the bar chart and decide what the title, key, labels and numbers mean.

3 Make notes or highlight the data you want to include in your summary:

opening statement	
main information	
comparison or contrast	

4 Write your summary. Try to include the language you practised in the exercises on pages 43–45. Use the ideas in the the task and title but avoid copying them word for word.

After you write

5 Read through what you have written.

Check for

- **meaning** – does it give correct information, according to the chart?
  - have you supported your ideas with data from the chart?
- **grammatical slips** – do your verbs agree with their subjects?
  - have you used the correct prepositions?
  - have you used articles correctly?, etc.
- **spelling** – have you copied words correctly?
  - have you avoided habitual mistakes?
- **length** – have you written at least 150 words?

6 Correct any mistakes neatly, but do not rewrite the whole essay.

Writing Task 1

You should spend about 20 minutes on this task.

The bar chart below gives information about the percentage of the population living in urban areas in different parts of the world.

Summarise the information by selecting and reporting the main features, and make comparisons where relevant.

Write at least 150 words.

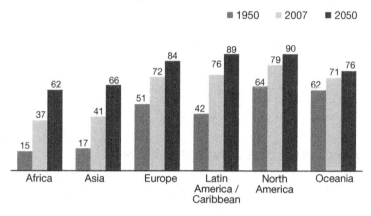

Changes in percentage of population in urban areas

■ 1950   ■ 2007   ■ 2050

What is Writing Task 2?

- a formal discussion essay

What does it test?

- expressing and evaluating ideas
- use of an appropriate style
- grammar, spelling and punctuation
- paragraphing

Task information

This task requires you to to present arguments in a clear and well-organised way.

You have to:

- write at least 250 words in 40 minutes.
- discuss the idea expressed in the task.
- give your opinion and support it with relevant examples.
- conclude with a brief statement of your final opinion.

STRATEGIES

Before you write

A   Reading the question

Read the task below and think about the questions in the boxes. This is the kind of task you will see in Writing Task 2.

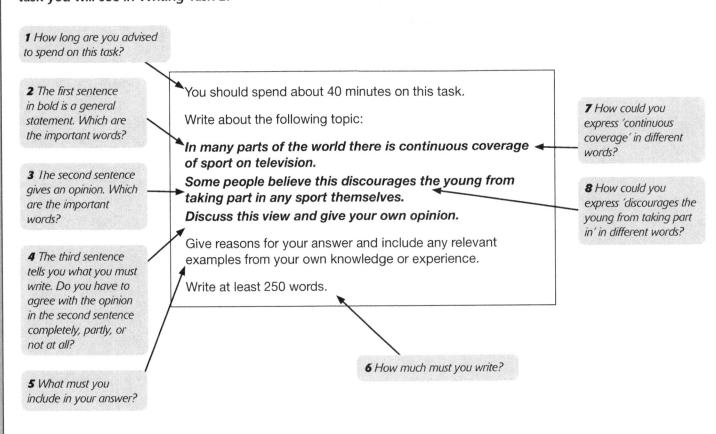

1 How long are you advised to spend on this task?

2 The first sentence in bold is a general statement. Which are the important words?

3 The second sentence gives an opinion. Which are the important words?

4 The third sentence tells you what you must write. Do you have to agree with the opinion in the second sentence completely, partly, or not at all?

5 What must you include in your answer?

You should spend about 40 minutes on this task.

Write about the following topic:

In many parts of the world there is continuous coverage of sport on television.
Some people believe this discourages the young from taking part in any sport themselves.
Discuss this view and give your own opinion.

Give reasons for your answer and include any relevant examples from your own knowledge or experience.

Write at least 250 words.

6 How much must you write?

7 How could you express 'continuous coverage' in different words?

8 How could you express 'discourages the young from taking part in' in different words?

B Planning your answer

Before you start writing your answer, it is essential to plan what you want to say and to organise it. This is one way of presenting your answer:

Stage 1	An **introduction** restating the view expressed in the question and giving a brief reaction to it
Stage 2	A **discussion** of why some people hold this view, with examples or comments supporting it and against it
Stage 3	Your own **opinion**, supported by **examples**
Stage 4	Your final **conclusion**

Match these notes for Writing Task 2 on page 48 to Stages 1–4 above.

a *some watch instead of taking part but not the young*
...Stage 4...

b *most countries, many TV channels, including sport – people obviously like it but watching sport not necessarily alternative to participating*

....

c *teachers/parents see teenagers watching TV sport, worry because not active but teens need to relax – exam pressure*

....

d *my neighbourhood, teenagers – lots of sport – admire sports stars on TV – want to emulate them but older people watch instead of playing – office workers, no exercise*

....

C Developing a clearly structured argument

Using the correct words and phrases to tie your ideas together gives your writing coherence and makes your ideas easy to follow.

1 Read this model answer and fill gaps 1–5 with expressions a–e, and gaps 6–10 with expressions f–j.

Nowadays, in most countries, there are numerous television channels to choose from and these include non-stop broadcasting of sport. **1** .... many people must be interested in watching sport throughout the day and night. However, **2** .... watching sport makes people less keen on participating in it. Teachers and parents may be concerned when they see teenagers spending time watching sport on television and fear that they are not active enough. While there may be some justification for this, **3** .... young people are often under pressure, for example to do well in exams. They need to relax and give their minds and bodies a break.

4 .... the young do not tend to watch sport rather than participating in it. The teenagers in my neighbourhood regularly play football after school and at weekends they play in matches or go to the tennis courts or the swimming pool. **5** .... they all support various famous clubs and admire sports stars. These stars are their role models and watching them on television encourages participation in sporting activities **6** .... the young try to emulate the people they admire.

7 .... I have observed that some older people spend their evenings and weekends in front of the television, following sports such as international golf or motor racing. **8** .... many of these are middle-aged men (it tends to be men) who spend their days sitting at a desk in an office and who get very little exercise **9** .... they need it more than most.

10 .... although I accept that there are some people who may be discouraged from participating in sport because they can watch it on television instead, in my view this does not generally apply to the young.

a it does not necessarily follow that

b Therefore it would appear that

c it is also true that

d As well as this,

e In my experience,

f By contrast,

g In conclusion,

h Moreover,

i in spite of the fact that

j because

2 Which of the stages 1–4 in Exercise B on page 49 takes up more than one paragraph in this answer? Why?

Useful language: style

1 Compare the language of A and B below. Which style is more suitable for an essay?

> **A**
>
> I think, from what I've seen, kids are getting more and more lazy.
>
> And this is because of the way grown-ups behave – they let their kids do nothing for much too long.

> **B**
>
> In my opinion, it is noticeable that children are becoming increasingly lazy.
>
> Moreover, this is a result of adult behaviour as children are permitted to remain inactive for longer than they should.

2 Here are some language features of A. Can you find examples of them?

1 short verb forms
2 informal vocabulary
3 using a dash (–) instead of a linking word
4 simple vocabulary
5 repetition for emphasis
6 a conjunction / linking word at the beginning of a sentence

3 Now look at B. Can you find examples of these language features?

1 noun instead of verb
2 passive verb
3 impersonal structure
4 formal vocabulary
5 modal verb
6 an adverb at the beginning of a sentence

4 ◉ Choose the most appropriate phrases in *italics* for use in an essay from these IELTS candidates' sentences.

1 If *you don't like / people dislike* sport, *you probably won't / they are unlikely to* do it.

2 *I think / As I see it*, 24-hour sports programmes *make no difference / don't matter*.

3 I liked watching football matches on *television / TV*, but I *rarely played / didn't play much*.

Useful language: impersonal structures

1 ◉ Find and correct the errors in these IELTS candidates' sentences.

1 This is true that in some countries people do not like tourism.

2 That is obviously necessary to prepare yourself for such activities.

3 There is no doubt true that the media play a role in our lives.

4 This is a fact that increasing numbers of young people are leaving home.

2 Explain the meaning of these impersonal phrases.

1 It is unfortunate that
2 It is undeniable that
3 It is understandable that
4 It is generally accepted that
5 It is regrettable that
6 It is frequently asserted that
7 It is often assumed that
8 It is no doubt true that

3 Now make sentences with the phrases in Exercise 2 above, using the ideas in this box, or your own.

> students / affordable accommodation
> children / cartoons
> music / universal language
> careless driving / accidents

Example

It is undeniable that students often have difficulty finding affordable accommodation.

Useful language: *the* and no article

⊙ When you check your essay, make sure that your use of articles is correct. Read these sentences from IELTS candidates' essays and write *the* or – in each gap.

1 We should not overemphasise .... importance of .... wealth.

2 Films, books and .... Internet can provide almost all of .... necessary information.

3 In conclusion, it is not .... money that can solve children's problems, but .... love and .... good teaching.

4 A high level of .... education and .... development of .... technology affects agricultural societies.

5 In conclusion, I find that .... advantages of .... international tourism outweigh .... disadvantages.

6 If .... governments had more effective policies for these children who grow up in .... poverty, ... children would have more chance to contribute to .... society.

Useful language: giving reasons

⊙ Look at the pairs of extracts from IELTS candidates' essays. Choose the correct one in each pair and underline the correct phrase.

1 a This is not true for a number of reasons.

  b This is not true because of a number of reasons.

2 a Some people have a wide knowledge of the world as a result from travelling.

  b Some people have a wide knowledge of the world as a result of travelling.

3 a In society today, by the advance of science and technology, people know more than they used to.

  b In society today, because of the advance of science and technology, people know more than they used to.

4 a They gave free educational materials to the children. So that the children were more likely to attend classes.

  b They gave free educational materials to the children so that the children were more likely to attend classes.

5 a I assume the reason of this is that media companies are producing better films nowadays.

  b I assume the reason for this is that media companies are producing better films nowadays.

6 a In those countries women's rights are more developed and, as a consequence, women are more fairly treated there.

  b In those countries women's rights are more developed, as a consequence, women are more fairly treated there.

Useful language: paragraphing

Read this essay by a strong IELTS candidate. It is a good answer. However, it does not have paragraphs, which will lose marks. Mark each place where you think she should start a new paragraph and write 'new para' in the margin. Explain your decisions.

IELTS candidate's essay

These days, it is noticeable that young people are becoming less interested in team games, sports and other forms of exercise. It is my belief that this is mainly because of our everyday work, which is increasingly sedentary. Besides, I think every person would admit that sitting and relaxing is much easier than moving and running and sweating. The question is, how much of this laziness is because of the sports programmes on television? From one point of view it could be true that these programmes make young people lazy. However, this may be because some people who like sport, and also like watching sports, are attracted to the television programmes and spend so much time watching sport that there is no spare time for them to participate themselves. By contrast, watching sport may encourage some other young people to take up sport, as these individuals might like that sport and consequently want to try it to see how it feels. Watching such programmes on television can make us feel that we want to be active, want to play basketball, or go swimming and so on. Thus, I would suggest that there are positive aspects of watching sports programmes. In my opinion, the fundamental issue is the reason why we like sport. Does an individual like sport merely as a spectator or as a participant? If the reason is simply the pleasure of watching other people playing volleyball or football or even dancing, that person will never want to be among those who take part. However, if a person enjoys being active and joining in, then sports programmes will never prevent this.

Tip! Do not attempt to learn model or sample answers and rewrite them in the exam. Your composition will not fit the task exactly, even if it is about a similar subject. The examiners can recognise a prepared answer and you will lose a lot of marks.

Before you write

1 Look at the task below and read the question carefully. The question that you have to answer is printed in **bold italics**, but remember to read all the rest of the question too.

2 Underline the important parts of the task.

Tip! You are marked on the quality of your English, not how good your ideas are.

3 Consider alternative language to express the ideas in the task.

Tip! You will lose marks if you copy the wording of the instructions. Use your own words.

4 Make notes on the task before you begin to write your essay. Your notes should cover the four essential points described in Exercise B on page 49: introduction; discussion of the view expressed; your own opinion; conclusion.

5 Now write your composition.

After you write

6 Read through your answer. Correct any mistakes neatly, but do not rewrite the whole essay.

7 Check for

- **overall structure** – have you included the four essential points?

- **paragraphing** – do you start a new paragraph for each new idea?

- **coherence** – have you linked your ideas together clearly?

- **style** – have you used appropriately formal language?

- **grammar, spelling and punctuation** – are your verb forms correct? Are your adverbs spelt correctly? Have you used capitals, apostrophes and full stops correctly?

- **your habitual errors** – what are these? (see Writing Task 1 page 43)

Tip! If you have forgotten to use paragraphs, mark them in the correct places and write 'new para' in the margin.

You should spend about 40 minutes on this task.
Write about the following topic:

In many parts of the world there is continuous coverage of sport on television. Some people believe this discourages the young from taking part in any sport themselves.
Discuss this view and give your own opinion.

Give reasons for your answer and include any relevant examples from your own knowledge or experience.

Write at least 250 words.

Tip! Allow at least five minutes for planning before you write and another five minutes for checking at the end.

Tip! If you don't have an opinion, invent one!

Speaking Part 1

What is Speaking Part 1?

- a short introductory conversation lasting 4–5 minutes

What does it test?

- your ability to talk about personal experiences and interests

> **Tip!** Don't forget to take your passport or ID card to the exam room!

Task information

You are required to answer questions about everyday topics.

You have to:

- talk about some aspects of your life such as your family and friends, home, studies/work, leisure activities, etc.

- answer each question appropriately – usually in one or two sentences.

Useful language: topics

The topics in Part 1 are usually things that you can talk about easily.

1 You may be asked about where you live. Think about your home town, city or village. What is it like? Underline any of the expressions below that you could use to talk about it. Make a note of other expressions you need.

City/Town etc.	(big) city (medium-sized) town (tiny) village port
Position	to the north/east etc. of ... in the mountains on the coast not far from ...
Description	the capital in a rural/industrial/commercial region has a population of ... famous for ...
Part of the city/town	in the centre (of) on the outskirts (of) in a suburb on a housing estate on a busy street in a built-up area
Building/Street etc.	convenient crowded quiet modern typical traditional friendly isolated
Countryside/Landscape	mountainous flat agricultural popular with tourists

2 Make similar tables for yourself with useful words and expressions for other topics, e.g. family and friends, leisure activities, food.

> **Tip!** In Part 1 you will be asked questions on topics which are very familiar. It's important not to memorise answers – just try and talk about the topic naturally.

3 Look at the questions about your home town on page 60 and practise saying the answers.

> **Tip!** Answer the questions you are asked. Your answers needn't be more than one or two sentences. Don't give a long speech in this Part.

Useful language: adding information to your answers

1 Look at these questions and answers about learning English (1–5).
For each possible answer in italics, underline the correct alternative.

   1 How long have you been learning English?

      Since six years. / <u>*For six years.*</u>

   2 Do most children learn English in your country?

      <u>*Yes, they do.*</u> */ Yes, they are.*

   3 What can you remember about your early lessons?

      <u>*They were fun*</u>*. / They were funny.*

   4 Have you studied any other languages?

      I have studied Spanish until I was 14. / <u>*I studied Spanish until I was 14.*</u>

   5 What advice would you give to someone who wants to start learning English?

      <u>*Go to a class.*</u> */ Go to the class.*

2 The answers in Exercise 1 are too short. Choose one piece of extra
information to add to each answer.

  5 **a** You learn much faster with a teacher and it's hard to be motivated on
your own.

  2 **b** We start learning when we are seven and most people continue until
they leave school. I think it's a good idea to start young.

  4 **c** Apart from English, we could choose between Spanish and Portuguese.
I chose Spanish but I've given it up now.

  1 **d** I started when I was ten years old.

  3 **e** Our teacher used to play a lot of games with us. But we had to work
hard too.

> **Tip!** Never answer questions with one word, or just *Yes* or *No*. Give an extra piece of
> information or a reason.

3 Look at the questions above about learning English and practise
answering them about yourself.

Speaking Part 2

What is Speaking Part 2?

- a short talk

What does it test?

- your ability to talk for about two minutes
- your ability to organise your ideas and speak fluently

Task information

You are required to prepare and talk about a topic given to you during the test by the examiner.

You have to:

- read a card with a task on it.
- make notes on each of the separate parts of the task. You have a minute or two to do this.
- talk about the topic in the task, answering the questions on the card.
- stop talking when the examiner tells you to.
- answer some follow-up questions.

Useful language: adjectives for describing people

Here are some characteristics you might admire in different people. Which other adjectives from the box could describe each of these people a–e? Write them in the gaps.

amusing   cheerful   considerate   courageous   determined   encouraging
entertaining   ~~imaginative~~   inventive   optimistic   reliable   sympathetic   witty

a a creative person   imaginative   _inventive_
b a funny person   _amusing_   _entertaining_   _witty_
c a kind person   _considerate_   _sympathetic_
d a positive person   _cheerful_   _encouraging_   _optimistic_
e a strong person   _courageous_   _reliable_   _determined_

Tip! Use a wide range of adjectives when you are describing someone or something.

Useful language: making notes

1 Look at the task on page 60. Underline the important words. Read the notes one candidate made for this task.

Tip! Use the preparation time to think about what you will say even if you don't write very much.

> <u>Who?</u> my brother, five years older
> <u>Kind of person?</u> fun, energetic, patient
> <u>Relationship?</u> cycling + fishing together during holidays, no time when busy (I got upset)
> <u>Influence?</u> balance work/play, gave me confidence

Think about what the candidate might say using the notes.

2 Look at the task on page 60 again and write some notes for yourself.

3 Here are some useful phrases you might want to use in your talk. Can you add any more?

> What I really admired about X was …
> X was a … kind of person
> I respected X because …
> The best times were …
> X made me feel …
> We used to …
> X inspired / encouraged / supported / stood up for me
> X was always there for me

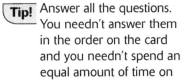 **Tip!** Answer all the questions. You needn't answer them in the order on the card and you needn't spend an equal amount of time on each one. You may have more to say about some questions than others.

Useful language: giving a talk

1 Make sure you introduce the topic. Here are some suggestions of ways to begin.

> The person / What I want to talk about is …
> I'd like to tell you about X …
> I've chosen to talk about …

2 Look at the notes you made in Making notes, Exercise 2. Record yourself talking for two minutes. Use a clock to time yourself.

3 Listen to what you said and think about how to improve it. Think about these questions.
- Did you introduce the topic?
- Did you use the correct tenses?
- Did you use a range of vocabulary?
- Did you connect your sentences?
- Did you cover all the points on the card (not necessarily in that order)?
- Did you speak clearly?

4 Look at the two follow-up questions on page 60 and think of your answers. You only need to give short answers to these.

5 Practise talking about the topics below for two minutes. Don't forget to make some notes and time yourself for each one.
- your favourite music and why you like it
- a special day, what you did, why it was important
- a place you have visited, why you went there, what you did and if you enjoyed it

Tip! You must talk about the topic on the card. Remember, what you say doesn't have to be completely true or exciting and you don't need any special knowledge.

Speaking Part 3

What is Speaking Part 3?

- a discussion of general and abstract ideas lasting 4–5 minutes

What does it test?

- your ability to analyse and discuss ideas in depth

Task information

You are required to answer questions which relate to the topic in Part 2.

You have to:

- offer your opinions and give reasons for them.

Useful language: giving opinions

There are errors in the phrases below used by IELTS candidates.
Correct the mistakes so that you have a list of expressions for giving your opinion.
(Sometimes there is more than one mistake in a phrase.)

1 ~~From~~ In my opinion, ...
2 As far as I am concerned for
3 There are several reasons about my opinion.
4 I strongly disagree with the idea that ...
5 I am completely agree to this opinion.
6 From the point of my view, ...

Here are some more expressions used by IELTS candidates. Three of these are not good English. Tick (✓) the ones you could use to give your opinion.

7 It seems to me that ...
8 According to my point of view, ...
9 It is my view that ...
10 In my own opinion, I think ...
11 Personally, I think that ...
12 What I think is that ...
13 According to me, ...

Useful language: easily confused words and expressions

1 Here are some examples of language used by IELTS candidates. Underline the correct word in italics in each sentence.

1 Parents should be more restricted / strict with their children.
2 Children who are grown up / brought up by working parents are more independent.
3 Children who live in extended / joint families tend to have better social skills.
4 A lot of children do not respect elder / elderly people because they have so little contact with them.
5 Children from sole / single parent families are often close to their grandparents.
6 Schools should punish children for bad behaviour / behaving.
7 Children whose parents let / allow them to do what they want learn to make their own rules.
8 Children who are spoilt do not learn how to behave in the society / society.

2 Read the statements in Exercise 1 again and decide if you agree or disagree with each one. Look at the task on page 60 and think about what you would say. Practise saying your answers.

Speaking Part 1

The examiner will ask you some questions about yourself.

Let's talk about your home town.

Where do you come from?
What is it like there?
Do you like living there?
Have you always lived there?
What is the countryside like near your home town?

The examiner will then ask you some questions about one or two other topics, for example:

Now let's talk about learning English.

How long have you been learning English?
Do most children learn English in your country?
What can you remember about your early lessons?
Have you studied any other languages? Which language do you find easier?
What advice would you give to someone who wants to start learning English?

Speaking Part 2

The examiner will give you a topic on a card like the one on the right and ask you to talk about it for one to two minutes. Before you talk you'll have one minute to think about what you're going to say. The examiner will give you some paper and a pencil so you can make notes if you want to.

The examiner may ask one or two more questions when you have finished, for example:

Did the person you've described influence other people too?
Are you similar to this person?

Speaking Part 3

The examiner will ask some more general questions which follow on from the topic in Part 2.

Do children nowadays have too many toys, electronic games and so on?
Do parents give their children toys instead of paying attention to them?
Is it the responsibility of parents or schools to teach children how to behave well?
Do children learn better if they have fun at school, or if the teachers are strict?
Do you think attitudes towards bringing up children differ in different parts of the world?
What about respect for older people, does that vary in different countries?

Tip! The Speaking test is recorded. This is just for administrative reasons.

Tip! Listen to the tense in the question so you use the right one in your answer.

> **Describe someone who influenced you when you were a child.**
> **You should say:**
> **who the person was**
> **what kind of person he/she was**
> **what your relationship was like**
> **and explain how he/she influenced you.**

Tip! The examiner will tell you when to start speaking.

Tip! The examiner may ask you some questions during your talk.

Tip! Don't worry if you haven't finished when the examiner tells you to stop.

Tip! You are given a mark across all three parts, not a different mark for each part separately.

Review

1 How many speakers will you hear?

2 How many times will you hear the recording?

3 How many questions do you have to answer?

4 Does each task in this section have the same number of questions?

5 Is there an example answer?

6 What information do you have to listen for in Section 1?

7 Do you have to write the exact words you hear?

8 Is spelling important in Section 1?

9 When do you transfer your answers to the answer sheet?

Action plan reminder

Form completion

1 How do you know how many words to write?

2 Do you have time to look at the task before you hear the recording?

3 What can you learn from the words around the gaps?

4 How can you lose marks in this task?

Page 13 *Test 1 Listening Section 1 Action plan*

 Questions 1–6

Complete the form below.

*Write **NO MORE THAN TWO WORDS** for each answer.*

PRIME RECRUITMENT
Employee record

Example	Answer
Surname	......Riley......

Email I .... @worldnet.com

Nationality 2 ....

Reference (professional) Name: John Keen
Job: manager of **3** ....

Reference (personal) Name: Eileen Dorsini
Job: **4** ....

Special qualifications current **5** .... certificate
certificate of competence in **6** ....

Tip! You don't have to write the same number of words in each space.

Tip! There is always an example in Listening Section 1 but not in the rest of the Listening test. As soon as you hear the answer to the example, listen for the answer to Question 1.

Advice

2 *Be careful to write a nationality, not the name of a country.*

3 *What kind of word(s) do you need here?*

4 *Is this the same kind of word as for Question 3?*

Action plan reminder

Table completion

1 How do you know how many words to write?

2 What should you check before the recording begins?

3 How will you know when an answer is coming?

◄ **Page 22** *Test 1 Listening Section 4 Action plan*

 Questions 7–10

Complete the table below.

Write **NO MORE THAN ONE WORD** *for each answer.*

Tip! You need a different number of words in this part!

PRIME RECRUITMENT CHILDCARE VACANCIES			
Location	**Name**	**Children**	**Special requirements**
London	Benton	girl and boy	be keen on 7 ....
near Oxford	Granger	8 .... boys	be animal-lover
9	Campbell	four girls	be willing to 10 .... when camping

Advice

7 *What kind of word is needed here?*

8 *This word probably indicates how many boys.*

9 *Be ready for a place name.*

10 *What kind of word do you need here?*

Review

1 How many speakers will you hear?

2 How many times will you hear the recording?

3 How many tasks are there usually?

4 How many questions do you have to answer?

5 Does each task have the same number of questions?

6 Is there an example?

7 What does Section 2 test?

Action plan for *Multiple choice (five options)*

1 Read the question(s) and the list of items A–E. This will give you an idea of what you will hear and what information you should listen for.

Tip! You will probably hear all the things A–E mentioned, but only TWO of them will be the correct answer for the questions.

2 Listen for the answers to each question.

3 There will be a pause during the recording at the end of the first task. During the pause read the questions in the second task.

◀ **Page 15** *Test 1 Listening Section 2 Action plan*

🎧 13 *Questions 11 and 12*

Choose **TWO** letters, **A–E**.

Which **TWO** sources of funding helped build the facility?

A	the central government
B	local government
C	a multinational company
D	a national company
E	city residents

Tip! You'll hear the information for Questions 11 and 12 before the information for Questions 13 and 14.

Advice

11 & 12 What is a 'source of funding'?

🎧 13 *Questions 13 and 14*

Choose **TWO** letters, **A–E**.

Which **TWO** pre-existing features of the site are now part of the new facilities?

A	football stadium
B	playing fields
C	passenger hall
D	control tower
E	aircraft hangars

Advice

13 & 14 What does 'pre-existing' mean? In what kind of place would you find things like C–E?

Action plan for *Map labelling*

1 Look at the map and read the instructions.

Tip! This task is similar to, but not exactly the same as, a diagram labelling task.

2 Try to understand what the map shows and how to describe the location of each of the places marked.

Tip! The letters on the map are *not* in the same order as the places you hear mentioned, but the places in the questions are in the right order.

3 Read the instructions, so you know what to write (e.g. a word or a letter).

4 Use the places already marked on the map to help you follow the recording.

5 Write the names of the places on the map as you listen.

6 Write the letters next to the question numbers at the end.

Tip! The speaker will say exactly where you are on the map at the beginning.

🎧13 Questions 15–20

Label the map below.

*Write the correct letter, **A–H**, next to questions 15–20.*

Tip! There are some letters on the map which you don't need to use.

15	hotel	....
16	transport hub	....
17	cinema	....
18	fitness centre	....
19	shops	....
20	restaurant	....

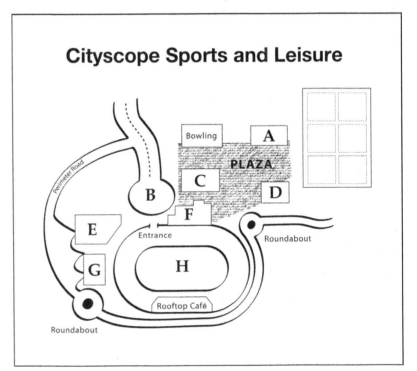

Cityscope Sports and Leisure

Review

1 Is the topic about academic situations or is it more general?

2 How many speakers are there?

3 How many times do you hear the recording?

4 How many questions do you have to answer?

5 Does each task have the same number of questions?

6 When are you given time to read the questions?

Action plan reminder

Multiple choice

1 Are the questions (21, 22, etc.) in the same order as the recording?

2 Are the options (A, B, C, etc.) in the same order as the recording?

3 How do you know the answer to the next question is coming?

4 What should you do before you listen?

Page 15 *Test 1 Listening Section 2 Action plan*

⏺ 14 *Questions 21–25*

*Choose the correct letter, **A, B** or **C**.*

21 What is Chloe concerned about?

    A   her knowledge of maths
    B   her ability to write essays
    C   her lack of business experience

22 Which of the following does Ivan feel he has improved?

    A   his computer skills
    B   his presentation skills
    C   his time management

23 What does Chloe especially like about the course?

    A   She won't have to do a final examination.
    B   She can spend time working in a business.
    C   She can study a foreign language.

24 Ivan is pleased that the university is going to have

    A   more lecture rooms.
    B   a larger library.
    C   more courses.

25 What does Ivan advise Chloe to do?

    A   contact his tutor
    B   read about some other universities
    C   visit the university

Tip! Read the questions to give you an idea of what the conversation is about.

Advice

Which speaker is thinking of doing the course? What kind of course is it?

21 What does Ivan say which tells you that you need to listen for the answer?

22 Ivan mentions all of the options but he only feels one has improved.

23 What words does Chloe use to say she especially likes something?

Action plan for *Matching A, B and C*

1 Read the options (A, B, C) you have to choose from.

2 Listen carefully to hear the words in the numbered questions, and decide which option from A, B and C is closest in meaning to what the speaker says.

3 Choose an answer to each of the questions. The questions are in the order you hear them.

Tip! There may sometimes be more than three options (A, B, C) to choose from.

 Questions 26–30

What does Chloe decide about the following subjects?

*Write the correct letter, **A**, **B** or **C**, next to questions 26–30.*

A	She will study it.
B	She won't study it.
C	She might study it.

Subjects

26 Public relations   ....

27 Marketing   ....

28 Taxation   ....

29 Human resources   ....

30 Information systems   ....

Tip! You have time to read the questions before you listen.

Advice

Only put A or B as your answer if Chloe is definite in what she says.

26 *Listen for Chloe's final opinion.*

27 *Chloe sometimes disagrees with Ivan about whether a course is useful or not.*

29 *What expression does Chloe use which matches A, B or C?*

30 *When a speaker makes a statement followed by 'but ...', listen carefully to what comes after 'but' as that will probably give you the answer.*

Review

1 How many speakers are there?
2 What kind of topic might you hear?
3 How many times do you hear the recording?
4 How many questions do you have to answer?
5 Does each task always have the same number of questions?
6 When are you given time to read the questions?

Action plan reminder

Note completion

1 Do you write the same number of words in each gap?
2 Are the gaps in the same order as the information you hear?

Tip! Use the information and the headings in the notes to find your place in the recording.

3 What should you think about when you look at the gaps?
4 Are the words you need all on the recording?
5 Do you have to spell the words correctly?

◀ **Page 13** *Test 1 Listening Section 1 Action plan*

 Questions 31–35

Complete the notes below.

*Write **NO MORE THAN TWO WORDS** for each answer.*

History of weather forecasting

Early methods

- Almanacs connected the weather with the positions of different **31** .... at particular times.

Invention of weather instruments

- A hygrometer showed levels of **32** .... (Nicholas Cusa 1450)
- Temperature variations first measured by a thermometer containing **33** .... (Galileo Galilei 1593)
- A barometer indicated air pressure (Evangelista Torricelli 1643)

Transmitting weather information

- The use of the **34** .... allowed information to be passed around the world.
- Daily **35** .... were produced by the French from 1863.

Advice

The lecture begins with an introduction. Which word tells you to listen for the first answer?

32 Check the words you write make sense. (The names and the dates will help you hear the answer.)

33 Be careful! The answer may not be what you expect from general knowledge.

Action plan reminder

Sentence completion

1 Do you write the same number of words in each gap?

2 Are the questions in the same order as the information you hear?

3 Are the words you need all on the recording?

◀ **Page 13** *Test 1 Listening Section 1 Action plan*

🎧 15 **Questions 36–40**

Complete the sentences below.

*Write **NO MORE THAN TWO WORDS** for each answer.*

Producing a weather forecast

36 Weather observation stations are found mostly at .... around the country.

37 Satellite images use the colour orange to show ....

38 The satellites give so much detail that meteorologists can distinguish a particular ....

39 Information about the upper atmosphere is sent from instruments attached to a ....

40 Radar is particularly useful for following the movement of ....

Tip! The second task will be on a different aspect of the first topic. The title will help you.

Advice

36 The word 'mostly' is important.

37 Listen for 'orange' which tells you the answer is coming.

39 Listen for a word which means 'instruments'.

Review

1 How many questions do you have to answer?
2 Does each task have the same number of questions?
3 How long should you spend on this passage?

NOW FOLLOW THE ACTION PLAN REMINDER ON PAGE 71

*You should spend about 20 minutes on **Questions 1–13**, which are based on Reading Passage 1 below.*

Our Vanishing Night
Most city skies have become virtually empty of stars
by Verlyn Klinkenborg

If humans were truly at home under the light of the moon and stars, it would make no difference to us whether we were out and about at night or during the day, the midnight world as visible to us as it is to the vast number of nocturnal species on this planet. Instead, we are diurnal creatures, meaning our eyes are adapted to living in the sun's light. This is a basic evolutionary fact, even though most of us don't think of ourselves as diurnal beings any more than as primates or mammals or Earthlings. Yet it's the only way to explain what we've done to the night: we've engineered it to meet our needs by filling it with light.

This kind of engineering is no different from damming a river. Its benefits come with consequences – called light pollution – whose effects scientists are only now beginning to study. Light pollution is largely the result of bad lighting design, which allows artificial light to shine outward and upward into the sky, where it is not wanted, instead of focusing it downward, where it is. Wherever human light spills into the natural world, some aspect of life – migration, reproduction, feeding – is affected.

For most of human history, the phrase 'light pollution' would have made no sense. Imagine walking toward London on a moonlit night around 1800, when it was one of Earth's most populous cities. Nearly a million people lived there, making do, as they always had, with candles and lanterns. There would be no gaslights in the streets or squares for another seven years.

Now most of humanity lives under reflected, refracted light from overlit cities and suburbs, from light-flooded roads and factories. Nearly all of night-time Europe is a bright patch of light, as is most of the United States and much of Japan. In the South Atlantic the glow from a single fishing fleet – squid fishermen luring their prey with metal halide lamps – can be seen from space, burning brighter on occasions than Buenos Aires.

 Tip! Read the title and subtitle which tell you what the topic is.

 Tip! Quickly skim the passage to get a general idea of what it is about and the topic of each paragraph. Don't worry about words you don't understand and don't spend too long trying to work out what they mean. If you read on, they may be explained anyway.

In most cities the sky looks as though it has been emptied of stars and taking their place is a constant orange glow. We've become so used to this that the glory of an unlit night – dark enough for the planet Venus to throw shadows on Earth – is wholly beyond our experience, beyond memory almost. And yet above the city's pale ceiling lies the rest of the universe, utterly undiminished by the light we waste.

We've lit up the night as if it were an unoccupied country, when nothing could be further from the truth. Among mammals alone, the number of nocturnal species is astonishing. Light is a powerful biological force, and on many species it acts as a magnet. The effect is so powerful that scientists speak of songbirds and seabirds being 'captured' by searchlights on land or by the light from gas flares on marine oil platforms, circling and circling in the thousands until they drop. Migrating at night, birds are apt to collide with brightly lit buildings; immature birds suffer in much higher numbers than adults.

Insects, of course, cluster around streetlights, and feeding on those insects is a crucial means of survival for many bat species. In some Swiss valleys the European lesser horseshoe bat began to vanish after streetlights were installed, perhaps because those valleys were suddenly filled with light-feeding pipistrelle bats. Other nocturnal mammals, like desert rodents and badgers, are more cautious about searching for food under the permanent full moon of light pollution because they've become easier targets for the predators who are hunting them.

Some birds – blackbirds and nightingales, among others – sing at unnatural hours in the presence of artificial light. Scientists have determined that long artificial days – and artificially short nights – induce early breeding in a wide range of birds. And because a longer day allows for longer feeding, it can also affect migration schedules. The problem, of course, is that migration, like most other aspects of bird behavior, is a precisely timed biological behavior. Leaving prematurely may mean reaching a destination too soon for nesting conditions to be right.

Nesting sea turtles, which seek out dark beaches, find fewer and fewer of them to bury their eggs on. When the baby sea turtles emerge from the eggs, they gravitate toward the brighter, more reflective sea horizon but find themselves confused by artificial lighting behind the beach. In Florida alone, hatchling losses number in the hundreds of thousands every year. Frogs and toads living on the side of major highways suffer nocturnal light levels that are as much as a million times brighter than normal, disturbing nearly every aspect of their behavior, including their night-time breeding choruses.

It was once thought that light pollution only affected astronomers, who need to see the night sky in all its glorious clarity. And, in fact, some of the earliest civic efforts to control light pollution were made half a century ago to protect the view from Lowell Observatory in Flagstaff, Arizona. In 2001 Flagstaff was declared the first International Dark Sky City. By now the effort to control light pollution has spread around the globe. More and more cities and even entire countries have committed themselves to reducing unwanted glare.

Action plan reminder

True/False/Not given

1 Will the questions focus on author opinion or factual information?

2 Are the questions in the same order as the information you need in the text?

3 Will there always be at least one True, one False and one Not given answer?

4 Is there an answer in every paragraph?

5 Look at the text. What will you do first?

6 Look at the questions. What will you do before you look for the answers?

◀ **Page 25** *Test 1 Reading Passage 1 Action plan*

Questions 1–7

Do the following statements agree with the information given in Reading Passage 1?

In boxes 1–7 on your answer sheet, write

TRUE	*if the statement agrees with the information*
FALSE	*if the statement contradicts the information*
NOT GIVEN	*if there is no information on this*

1   Few people recognise nowadays that human beings are designed to function best in daylight.

2   Most light pollution is caused by the direction of artificial lights rather than their intensity.

3   By 1800 the city of London had such a large population, it was already causing light pollution.

4   The fishermen of the South Atlantic are unaware of the light pollution they are causing.

5   Shadows from the planet Venus are more difficult to see at certain times of year.

6   In some Swiss valleys, the total number of bats declined rapidly after the introduction of streetlights.

7   The first attempts to limit light pollution were carried out to help those studying the stars.

Tip! Use the words in the statements to find the part of the text you need to read carefully for each question. Remember – the text may use different words from the questions.

Tip! If you find the right part of the text but you can't find the answer, the answer is 'Not given'.

Advice

1 The first paragraph is about human beings in general. Underline the sentence about how most of us think of ourselves.

2 The text mentions 'bad lighting design'. Does this refer to how strong the lights are or which way they point?

3 Find the paragraph about London in 1800. Read the whole paragraph and then answer the question.

4 Find the part of the text about fishermen. What does it say about their awareness of light pollution?

5 Find the paragraph which mentions Venus. What does it say about when we can see the shadows?

6 Find the part of the text which mentions Swiss valleys. Read about both kinds of bats to get the right answer.

7 Look at the paragraph about astronomers. Find the words which mean 'the first attempts to limit light pollution' and read the rest of the sentence. The first sentence and 'in fact' also help you to answer the question.

Action plan reminder

Table completion

1 What important information do the instructions give you?

2 What should you think about when you look at the gaps?

3 Are the words you need all in the text?

4 Can you change words or use different words with the same meaning for your answer?

5 Do you have to spell the words correctly?

 Page 27 *Test 1 Reading Passage 1 Action plan*

Questions 8–13

Complete the table below.

*Choose **NO MORE THAN THREE WORDS** from the passage for each answer.*

Write your answers in boxes 8–13 on your answer sheet.

CREATURE	EFFECTS OF LIGHT
Songbirds and seabirds	The worst-affected birds are those which are 8 .... They bump into 9 .... which stand out at night.
Desert rodents and badgers	They are more at risk from 10 ....
Migrating birds	Early migration may mean the 11 .... are not suitable on arrival.
Sea turtles	They suffer from the decreasing number of 12 ....
Frogs and toads	If they are near 13 .... , their routines will be upset.

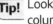 When you have completed the table, read it through. Do your answers make sense? For example, in 8, 11 and 12 you need an adjective as well as a noun.

Tip! Look at the headings of the columns. For each kind of creature you are going to look at the ways they are affected by light.

Tip! For each question find the part of the text which is about those creatures. They are in the same order as the text.

Tip! Some of the words you need will be singular and some will be plural. Copy them carefully.

Advice

Do all the gaps need nouns or noun phrases?

8 Which words mean 'worst-affected'?

9 Which paragraph is about songbirds and seabirds? Which word means 'bump into'? Why are 'searchlights' and 'oil platforms' wrong?

10 There is one sentence about desert rodents and badgers. Which words say they are 'at risk'?

11 Which paragraph is about migration? Which words mean 'on arrival'? What does the text say is not suitable?

12 There are three sentences about sea turtles. What is there a lack of? Which words tell you? Does this make the turtles suffer? Why is 'artificial lighting' wrong?

13 Which paragraph is about frogs and toads? Which words in the text mean 'their routines will be upset'? What are they near when this happens?

Review

1 How many questions do you have to answer?

2 Does each task have the same number of questions?

3 How long should you spend on this section?

Action plan for *Matching paragraph headings*

Tip! If there is a *Matching paragraph headings* task, it is always before the text to encourage you to read the headings before you read the text.

1 Check how many headings there are and how many paragraphs there are in the text.

2 Read the first paragraph of the text quickly. Underline the main ideas and choose the best heading.

3 Do the same for the other paragraphs. You can only use each heading once.

Tip! If you are not sure about one paragraph, do the rest of the task and go back when you haven't got so many headings to choose from.

*You should spend about 20 minutes on **Questions 14–26**, which are based on Reading Passage 2 on pages 74–75.*

Questions 14–20

Reading Passage 2 has seven paragraphs, *A–G*.

*Choose the correct heading for **A–G** from the list of headings below.*

Tip! The headings are about the main ideas in each paragraph, not about one or two details.

*Write the correct number, **i–x**, in boxes 14–20 on your answer sheet.*

List of Headings

i	A comparison between similar buildings
ii	The negative reaction of local residents
iii	An unusual job for a psychologist
iv	A type of building benefiting from prescribed guidelines
v	The need for government action
vi	A failure to use available information in practical ways
vii	Academics with an unhelpful attitude
viii	A refusal by architects to accept criticism
ix	A unique co-operative scheme
x	The expanding scope of environmental psychology

14 Paragraph **A**
15 Paragraph **B**
16 Paragraph **C**
17 Paragraph **D**
18 Paragraph **E**
19 Paragraph **F**
20 Paragraph **G**

Advice

14 *Whose response surprised Chris Spencer?*

15 *Does Paragraph B focus on a particular situation or a general one?*

Is there a psychologist in the building?

— *CHRISTIAN JARRETT reports on psychology's place in new architectural development.* —

A The space around us affects us profoundly – emotionally, behaviourally, cognitively. In Britain that space is changing at a pace not seen for a generation. Surely psychology has something to say about all this change. But is anyone listening? 'There is a huge amount of psychology research that is relevant, but at the moment we're talking to ourselves,' says Chris Spencer, professor of environmental psychology at the University of Sheffield. Spencer recalls a recent talk he gave in which he called on fellow researchers to make a greater effort to communicate their findings to architects and planners. 'I was amazed at the response of many of the senior researchers, who would say: "I'm doing my research for pure science, the industry can take it or leave it". But there are models of how to apply environmental psychology to real problems, if you know where to look. Professor Frances Kuo is an example.

B Kuo's website provides pictures and plain English summaries of research conducted by her Human Environment Research Laboratory. Among these is a study using police records that found inner-city Chicago apartment buildings surrounded by more vegetation suffered 52 per cent fewer crimes than apartment blocks with little or no greenery. Frances Kuo and her co-researcher William Sullivan believe that greenery reduces crime – so long as visibility is preserved – because it reduces aggression, brings local residents together outdoors, and the conspicuous presence of people deters criminals.

C 'Environmental psychologists are increasingly in demand,' says David Uzzell, professor of environmental psychology. 'We're asked to contribute to the planning, design and management of many different environments, ranging from neighbourhoods, offices, schools, health, transport, traffic and leisure environments for the purpose of improving quality of life and creating a better people–environment fit.' Uzzell points to the rebuilding of one south London school as a striking example of how building design can affect human behaviour positively. Before its redesign, it was ranked as the worst school in the area – now it is recognised as one of the country's twenty most improved schools.

D Uzzell has been involved in a pioneering project between MSc students in England and Scotland. Architecture students in Scotland acted as designers while environmental psychology students in England acted as consultants, as together they worked on a community project in a run-down area of Glasgow. 'The psychology students encouraged the architecture students to think about who their client group was, to consider issues of crowding and social cohesion, and they introduced them to psychological methodologies, for example observation and interviewing local residents about their needs.' The collaborative project currently stands as a one-off experiment. 'Hopefully these trainee architects will now go away with some understanding of the psychological issues involved in design and will take into account people's needs,' says Uzzell.

E Hilary Barker, a recent graduate in psychology, now works for a design consultancy. She's part of a four-person research team that contributes to the overall work of the company in helping clients use their office space more productively. Her team all have backgrounds in psychology or social science, but the rest of the firm consists mainly of architects and interior designers. 'What I do is pretty rare to be honest,' Barker says. 'I feel very privileged to be able to use my degree in such a way.' Barker explains that the team carries out observational studies on behalf of companies, to identify exactly how occupants are using their building. The companies are often surprised by the findings, for example that staff use meeting rooms for quiet, individual work.

F One area where the findings from environment–behaviour research have certainly influenced building is in hospital design. 'The government has a checklist of criteria that must be met in the design of new hospitals, and these are derived largely from the work of the behavioural scientist Professor Roger Ulrich,' Chris Spencer says. Ulrich's work has shown, for example, how the view from a patient's window can affect their recovery. Even a hospital's layout can impact on people's health, according to Dr John Zeisel. 'If people get lost in hospitals, they get stressed, which lowers their immune system and means their medication works less well. You might think that way-finding round the hospital is the responsibility of the person who puts all the signs up, but the truth is that the basic layout of a building is what helps people find their way around,' he says.

G Zeisel also points to the need for a better balance between private and shared rooms in hospitals. 'Falls are reduced and fewer medication errors occur' in private rooms, he says. There's also research showing how important it is that patients have access to the outdoors and that gardens in hospitals are a major contributor to well-being. However, more generally, Zeisel shares Chris Spencer's concerns that the lessons from environmental psychology research are not getting through. 'There is certainly a gap between what we in social science know and the world of designers and architects,' says Zeisel. He believes that most industries, from sports to film-making, have now recognised the importance of an evidence-based approach, and that the building trade needs to formulate itself more in that vein, and to recognise that there is relevant research out there. 'It would be outrageous, silly, to go ahead with huge building projects without learning the lessons from the new towns established between 30 and 40 years ago,' he warns.

Action plan for *Selecting two answers from multiple choice (five-option)*

1 Read the question carefully and make sure you understand what you have to look for. Underline the important words.

2 Scan the text quickly. Find a reference in the text to each option and check to see if it answers the question. You only have to find two so don't keep checking if you are satisfied you have found the answers.

Tip! Some of the options may be close together and there may be some parts of the text you don't need to look at.

3 When you have found the answers, write the letters.

Questions 21 and 22

Choose **TWO** *letters,* **A–E.**

Write the correct letters in boxes 21 and 22 on your answer sheet.

Which **TWO** of the following benefits are said to arise from the use of environmental psychology when planning buildings?

    A   better relationships between staff

    B   improved educational performance

    C   reduction of environmental pollution

    D   fewer mistakes made by medical staff

    E   easier detection of crime

Tip! The options A–E are in the order that they appear in the text.

Advice

A What does research find out about office staff?

B In the parts of the text which refer to schools and universities, is improved educational performance mentioned?

C Does the text refer to levels of pollution in the environment?

D Which paragraphs talk about hospitals?

E What positive point is made about crime in the text?

Questions 23 and 24

Choose **TWO** *letters,* **A–E.**

Write the correct letters in boxes 23 and 24 on your answer sheet.

Which **TWO** of the following research methods are mentioned in the passage?

    A   the use of existing data relating to a geographical area

    B   measuring the space given to a variety of activities

    C   watching what people do in different parts of a building

    D   analysing decisions made during the planning of a building

    E   observing patients' reactions to each other

Advice

Each option **A–E** *describes a research method and its context. When you choose your answers, make sure the whole statement is correct.*

Action plan for *Sentence completion*

1 Look at the instructions and check how many words you must write.

2 Underline key words in each sentence. Decide what kinds of word you need for each gap (e.g. noun, adjective, etc.).

3 The sentences follow the order of the information in the text. Find the part of the text you need for each one.

4 Mark the words you need in the text.

5 Copy them exactly and make sure you spell correctly.

Questions 25–26

Complete the sentences below.

*Choose **NO MORE THAN TWO WORDS** from the passage for each answer.*

Write your answers in boxes 25 and 26 on your answer sheet.

25 The students from England suggested that the Scottish students should identify their ....

26 John Zeisel believes that if the .... of a building is clear, patient outcomes will improve.

Advice

25 *You need two words here.*

26 *Think about the meaning of 'patient outcomes' before looking for the answer.*

Review

1 How many tasks are there usually in this part?
2 Does each task have the same number of questions?
3 How long should you spend on this passage?

NOW FOLLOW THE ACTION PLAN REMINDER ON PAGE 80

*You should spend about 20 minutes on **Questions 27–40**, which are based on Reading Passage 3 below.*

Have teenagers always existed?

The development of humans

Our ancestor, *Homo erectus*, may not have had culture or even language, but did they have teenagers? That question has been contested in the past few years, with some anthropologists claiming evidence of an adolescent phase in human fossil. This is not merely an academic debate. Humans today are the only animals on Earth to have a teenage phase, yet we have very little idea why. Establishing exactly when adolescence first evolved and finding out what sorts of changes in our bodies and lifestyles it was associated with could help us understand its purpose. Why do we, uniquely, have a growth spurt so late in life?

Until recently, the dominant explanation was that physical growth is delayed by our need to grow large brains and to learn all the behaviour patterns associated with humanity – speaking, social interaction and so on. While such behaviour is still developing, humans cannot easily fend for themselves, so it is best to stay small and look youthful. That way your parents and other members of the social group are motivated to continue looking after you. What's more, studies of mammals show a strong relationship between brain size and the rate of development, with larger-brained animals taking longer to reach adulthood. Humans are at the far end of this spectrum. If this theory is correct, and the development of large brains accounts for the teenage growth spurt, the origin of adolescence should have been with the evolution of our own species (*Homo sapiens*) and Neanderthals, starting almost 200,000 years ago. The trouble is, some of the fossil evidence seems to tell a different story.

The human fossil record is extremely sparse, and the number of fossilised children minuscule. Nevertheless, in the past few years anthropologists have begun to look at what can be learned of the lives of our ancestors from these youngsters. One of the most studied is the famous Turkana boy, an almost complete skeleton of *Homo erectus* from 1.6 million years ago found in Kenya in 1984. Accurately assessing how old someone is from their skeleton is a tricky business. Even with a modern human, you can only make a rough estimate based on the developmental stage of teeth and bones and the skeleton's general size.

You need as many developmental markers as possible to get an estimate of age. The Turkana boy's teeth made him 10 or 11 years old. The features of his skeleton put him at 13, but he was as tall as a modern 15-year-old. Susan Anton of New York University points to research by Margaret Clegg who studied a collection of 18th- and 19th-century skeletons whose ages at death were known. When she tried to age the skeletons without checking the records, she found similar discrepancies to those of the Turkana boy. One 10-year-old boy, for example, had a dental age of 9, the skeleton of a 6-year-old but was tall enough to be 11. 'The Turkana kid still has a rounded skull, and needs more growth to reach the adult shape,' Anton adds. She thinks that *Homo erectus* had already developed modern human patterns of growth, with a late, if not quite so extreme, adolescent spurt. She believes Turkana boy was just about to enter it.

If Anton is right, that theory contradicts the orthodox idea linking late growth with development of a large brain. Anthropologist Steven Leigh from the University of Illinois goes further. He believes the idea of adolescence as catch-up growth does not explain why the growth rate increases so dramatically. He says that many apes have growth spurts in particular body regions that are associated with reaching maturity, and this makes sense because by timing the short but crucial spells of maturation to coincide with the seasons when food is plentiful, they minimise the risk of being without adequate food supplies while growing. What makes humans unique is that the whole skeleton is involved. For Leigh, this is the key.

According to his theory, adolescence evolved as an integral part of efficient upright locomotion, as well as to accommodate more complex brains. Fossil evidence suggests that our ancestors first walked on two legs six million years ago. If proficient walking was important for survival, perhaps the teenage growth spurt has very ancient origins. While many anthropologists will consider Leigh's theory a step too far, he is not the only one with new ideas about the evolution of teenagers.

Another approach, which has produced a surprising result, relies on the minute analysis of tooth growth. Every nine days or so the growing teeth of both apes and humans acquire ridges on their enamel surface. These are like rings in a tree trunk: the number of them tells you how long the crown of a tooth took to form. Across mammals, the rate at which teeth develop is closely related to how fast the brain grows and the age you mature. Teeth are good indicators of life history because their growth is less related to the environment and nutrition than is the growth of the skeleton.

A more decisive piece of evidence came last year, when researchers in France and Spain published their findings from a study of Neanderthal teeth. Neanderthals had much faster tooth growth than *Homo erectus* who went before them, and hence, possibly, a shorter childhood. Lead researcher Fernando Ramirez-Rozzi thinks Neanderthals died young – about 25 years old – primarily because of the cold, harsh environment they had to endure in glacial Europe. They evolved to grow up quicker than their immediate ancestors. Neanderthals and *Homo erectus* probably had to reach adulthood fairly quickly, without delaying for an adolescent growth spurt. So it still looks as though we are the original teenagers.

Action plan reminder

Multiple choice

1 What do you have to choose?

2 How many correct options are there for each question?

3 Are the questions in the same order as the ideas in the text?

4 If this is the first task, what should you do before you look at the questions?

5 Should you read and answer each question in turn?

6 How much of the text should you read for each question?

7 Can you answer the questions using your general knowledge?

 Page 38 *Test 1 Reading Passage 3 Action plan*

Questions 27–30

*Choose the correct letter, **A**, **B**, **C** or **D**.*

Write the correct letter in boxes 27–30 on your answer sheet.

Tip! Read the text quickly. Then read it more carefully as you answer each question in turn. Some paragraphs don't have a multiple-choice question on them.

27 In the first paragraph, why does the writer say 'This is not merely an academic debate'?

    A Anthropologists' theories need to be backed up by practical research.

    B There have been some important misunderstandings among anthropologists.

    C The attitudes of anthropologists towards adolescence are changing.

    D The work of anthropologists could inform our understanding of modern adolescence.

Advice

27 *Some questions tell you which paragraph to look at. You need to find the quoted sentence and then read the whole paragraph to find the answer.*

28 What was Susan Anton's opinion of the Turkana boy?

    A He would have experienced an adolescent phase had he lived.

    B His skull showed he had already reached adulthood.

    C His skeleton and teeth could not be compared to those from a more modern age.

    D He must have grown much faster than others alive at the time.

29 What point does Steven Leigh make?

    A Different parts of the human skeleton develop at different speeds.

    B The growth period of many apes is confined to times when there is enough food.

    C Humans have different rates of development from each other depending on living conditions.

    D The growth phase in most apes lasts longer if more food is available.

30 What can we learn from a mammal's teeth?

    A A poor diet will cause them to grow more slowly.

    B They are a better indication of lifestyle than a skeleton.

    C Their growing period is difficult to predict accurately.

    D Their speed of growth is directly related to the body's speed of development.

Action plan reminder

Yes/No/Not given

1 What do the statements focus on?

2 What must you decide?

3 How can you get an idea of who or what the text is about?

4 Should you worry about words you don't understand?

5 Are the statements in the same order as the text?

6 Look at the questions. What will you do before you look for the answers?

◀ Page 37 *Test 1 Reading Passage 3 Action plan*

Questions 31–36

Do the following statements agree with the claims of the writer in Reading Passage 3?

In boxes 31–36 on your answer sheet, write

YES	*if the statement agrees with the claims of the writer*
NO	*if the statement contradicts the claims of the writer*
NOT GIVEN	*if it is impossible to say what the writer thinks about this*

Tip! For each question, find the key words (or paraphrases of them) in the text, then read that part carefully to see what the writer claims.

31 It is difficult for anthropologists to do research on human fossils because they are so rare.

32 Modern methods mean it is possible to predict the age of a skeleton with accuracy.

33 Susan Anton's conclusion about the Turkana boy reinforces an established idea.

34 Steven Leigh's ideas are likely to be met with disbelief by many anthropologists.

35 Researchers in France and Spain developed a unique method of analysing teeth.

36 There has been too little research comparing the brains of *Homo erectus* and Neanderthals.

Advice

31 What do you find out about human fossils from the words 'sparse' and 'minuscule'?

34 What does 'a step too far' mean? Is this what many anthropologists think?

35 What does the text say about the methods used by researchers in France and Spain?

Action plan reminder

Matching sentence endings

1 How will you find the information you need?

2 Is the information in one part of the passage only?

3 Are the sentence beginnings in the same order as the information in the text?

4 Can you use a sentence ending more than once?

 Page 39 *Test 1 Reading Passage 3 Action plan*

Questions 37–40

*Complete each sentence with the correct ending, **A–G**, below.*

*Write the correct letter, **A–G**, in boxes 37–40 on your answer sheet.*

 Tip! For each sentence beginning, underline the important words and find the part of the text you need to read.

37 Until recently, delayed growth in humans until adolescence was felt to be due to

38 In her research, Margaret Clegg discovered

39 Steven Leigh thought the existence of adolescence is connected to

40 Research on Neanderthals suggests that they had short lives because of

Tip! When you have finished, read the whole sentences and make sure they say the same as the text.

A	inconsistencies between height, skeleton and dental evidence.
B	the fact that human beings walk on two legs.
C	the way teeth grew.
D	a need to be dependent on others for survival.
E	difficult climatic conditions.
F	increased quantities of food.
G	the existence of much larger brains than previously.

Review

1 What information is Writing Task 1 based on?
2 How do you have to express the information?
3 Does it matter whether you use an informal style?
4 Are grammar, spelling and punctuation tested?
5 How long should you spend on this task?

6 How many words must you write?
7 Which parts of the data must you write about?
8 Should you make comparisons?
9 What should you draw attention to and interpret?

Useful language: the introduction

1 **Read carefully these five introductions (1–5) to the task on page 87 written by IELTS candidates. Then answer questions a and b for each introduction.**

   a **Does the candidate give enough information about the table?**
   b **Does the candidate describe the information in the table accurately?**

   1 In the table we can see some information about students enrolled at Bristol University from the year 1928 till 2008.
   2 The table shows the numbers of student enrolments at Bristol University, covering the number of students, the percentages of female and male, and where they came from, in three different years.
   3 This table shows the number of people who are studying at Bristol University and the number of people of each gender as well. Also, it shows the distance that students come from, divided into two categories: within 30 miles of Bristol and overseas.
   4 The table illustrates some information about student enrolments at Bristol University. The table shows the percentages of male and female students and how many students came from overseas or within 30 miles of Bristol in 1928, 1958 and 2008.
   5 The table gives information about Bristol University student enrolments, the percentages of males and females and what area they came from, in the years 1928, 1958 and 2008.

2 **Suggest any improvements you could make to the content of each introduction. (There are no language errors.)**

3 **Underline any useful words or phrases drawing attention to important data that you might use when writing about other topics.**

Useful language: drawing attention to important data

1 👁 These sentences were written by IELTS candidates to describe different graphs and tables. Underline the words in each one that you could use in writing about other topics.

1 *Also noteworthy is the low government expenditure on education.*

2 *This graph shows a striking difference between the younger age group and the older one.*

3 *The most striking feature of the graph is the sudden increase in the popularity of computer games.*

4 *Another fact worth noticing in the table is that females are more numerous than males.*

5 *The most remarkable point is that the number of males with a criminal record increased dramatically.*

6 *It is noticeable that expenditure on photography remained stable from 1992 to 2000.*

2 Using the sentences in Exercise 1 as models, expand these notes into full sentences.

1 noteworthy / fall in graduate numbers
2 striking similarity / teenagers in the USA / teenagers in South America
3 most striking feature / sudden decline / birth rate
4 fact worth noticing / high cost / fossil fuels
5 most remarkable / growth rate / increased suddenly
6 noticeable / few schools / swimming pools

Useful language: numbers and percentages

1 👁 Be careful to use the appropriate nouns to report different kinds of number. Choose the correct word in these IELTS candidates' answers.

1 In 1997 the employment *figure/number* was two million.
2 The data shows the difference between the *percentage/percentages* of men and women doing full-time jobs.
3 In future the *size/number* of the population will increase sharply.
4 In Britain people spent the smallest *number/amount* of money on personal stereos.
5 Cinemas expect an increasing *level/number* of attendance in the future across all ages.
6 Going out to restaurants decreased dramatically to seven *percentage/per cent*.
7 The *number/quantity* of people who came to Australia started to drop after 1994.
8 The graph shows that the *percentage/per cent* of 14- to 24-year-olds who are cinema-goers is higher than other groups.
9 We can also see that the *rate/proportion* of males gaining diplomas was higher than that of females.
10 A small *part/proportion* of graduates are self-employed.
11 It can be seen that the majority of prisoners are male as the *percentage/share* of prisoners who are female is only 4%.
12 The number of books published depends on the literacy *rate/figure*.

2 Write sentences using phrases 1–7 and the words in brackets.

 Page 45 *Test 1 Writing Task 1 for useful verbs*

1 the rate of unemployment (1979 and 1985)

Unemployment

2 the proportion of the population (computers)

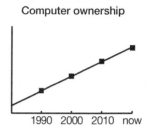

Computer ownership

1990 2000 2010 now

3 the amount of energy (industry)

Industrial energy consumption

1980s 1990s

4 the number of cars (public transport)

Car use

Public transport prices

5 the level of literacy (change of government)

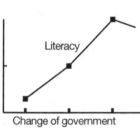

Literacy

Change of government

6 the quantity of food (affluent parts of the world)

Food waste

1960 1980 2000

7 the share of global resources (the poorest countries)

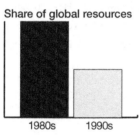

Share of global resources

1980s 1990s

Useful language: spelling

These sentences contain 22 of the most common spelling mistakes made by IELTS candidates. How fast can you find and correct them?

Give yourself one mark for spotting each mistake, another mark for putting it right correctly and deduct one mark for any changes you make to words that were not wrong!

1 Nowdays, knowladge about the enviroment is essencial and many goverments understand the benifits of educating childen to be aware of how they can contribute to this.

2 In my experiense, becouse sociaty is in some respects organised diffrently in other contries, foriegners find it relaxing to visit this part of the world.

3 It is my oppinion that few people beleive the information wich is given in advertisments.

4 Teenagers shoud not be allowed to have there own cars untill they are prepared to accept responsability for the affect that bad driving can have on other road users.

Useful language: finishing your summary

Here are four ways (1–4) used by IELTS candidates to finish their summaries for the task on page 87. Although there are no language errors, three of them are unsatisfactory for various reasons. Read the comments in the box and match them to the paragraphs.

a   Not an accurate description of what the table shows.
b   Statements should be supported by figures from the table.
c   Too vague. It is unclear what part of the data is referred to, and offers no conclusion.
d   A useful contrast, well supported by data from the table.

1   In conclusion, the percentage increased in different ways until 2008 and fell in other ways.

2   It is clear that the number of foreign students increased whereas the students who came from within 30 miles of Bristol decreased. Furthermore, in 2008 the number of female students who enrolled at the university was much higher than in 1928.

3   Finally, the figures for student enrolment at Bristol University changed dramatically. The number of students reached a peak in 1958 but went down again between the years 1958 and 2008. Overall, the number of foreign students remained almost the same between 1928 and 1958. However, it rose sharply in the next 50 years.

4   Lastly, there is an important difference in the proportion of students who come from within 30 miles of Bristol and those who come from overseas: at the beginning there were few students coming from overseas and more coming from near the city, while by 2008 the percentage of 'local' students had really decreased (from 50% to 1–2%), whereas the percentage of overseas students had increased from only 5% to 28%.

Action plan reminder

1 Look at Writing Task 1 below.
- What does the first part of the question tell you?
- What three things does the rest of the question remind you to do?

2 Look at the table in Writing Task 1 below.
- What do you learn from the title of this table?
- What do the headings of the three columns tell you?
- What information does the table contain?
- What do the numbers in the first row represent?
- Why is the second row divided into two smaller rows?
- Why do the bottom two rows not add up to 100%?

Before you write

3 Select data and highlight or make notes before you begin to write your summary.

4 Write your summary.
- What should you avoid copying word for word?
- Should you try to write about all the data?
- Should you challenge the data?

After you write

5 What should you check for when you have finished?

◄ **Page 40** *Test 1 Writing Task 1*

You should spend about 20 minutes on this task.

Tip! Remember you'll need more time for Task 2 than Task 1.

> *The table below gives information about student enrolments at Bristol University in 1928, 1958 and 2008.*
>
> *Summarise the information by selecting and reporting the main features, and make comparisons where relevant.*

Write at least 150 words.

Tip! Don't lose marks by writing too little.

Bristol University student enrolments			
	1928	**1958**	**2008**
How many new students enrolled?	218	1,046	6,377
What percentage were female?	42%	32%	54%
What percentage were male?	58%	68%	46%
What percentage came from within 30 miles of Bristol?	50%	14%	1–2%
What percentage came from overseas?	5% from 3 countries	6% from 27 countries	28% from 98 countries

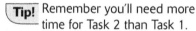

Advice

Between which years was the increase in enrolments greater?

When was the percentage of female enrolments lowest?

When did the percentage of overseas students change most markedly?

Review

1 What is Writing Task 2?
2 Which of these things does it test?
  - general knowledge
  - expressing ideas
  - having the correct opinions
  - evaluating ideas
  - academic knowledge
  - appropriate style
  - grammar
  - spelling
  - punctuation
  - paragraphing

3 How many words must you write?
4 How should you support your opinion?
5 How should you conclude your essay?

Useful language: conditionals

1 ⊙ **Choose the correct form of the verbs in italics in these sentences written by IELTS candidates.**

1 If people *would have / had* fun doing shopping, more people *will do / would do* it.

2 If shopping *was / would be* a routine domestic task in earlier times, this *could be / had been* because there was no interesting shopping to do.

3 This change *may be regarded / is regarded* as positive if we *will analyse / analyse* why it has happened.

4 People *spend / are spending* less time shopping if they *have / had* more enjoyable activities to do.

2 **Match these descriptions to the sentences in Exercise 1.**

a offering an explanation for a possible situation in the past
b imagining the necessary conditions for something to happen
c stating a generally accepted fact
d describing the possible result of doing something

3 ⊙ **Here are some sentences written by IELTS candidates. Put the verbs in brackets into the correct form. (Sometimes more than one answer is possible.)**

1 Human beings .... (have) the right to express their own ideas, unless they break the rules of our society.

2 Therefore, if I were a mother I .... (not give) my children money.

3 It would be better if sports professionals .... (not earn) a lot of money from other activities.

4 If they .... (be) richer, they could have afforded health care.

5 I wondered whether the people in the disaster area .... (deal) better with the situation if they had experienced hardships growing up.

6 Children may think that if they .... (bring up) by rich parents, they could get what they want very easily.

7 Had anyone given him the chance to rest, he .... (be) more relaxed in mind and body.

Useful language: referring to people

⊙ These are some examples of language written by IELTS candidates. Choose the correct word in italics in each sentence. After checking your answers, use the other word in each pair in a sentence of your own.

1 If the company's *consumers/customers* are satisfied, they are likely to come back.

2 Successful businessmen and women have to do better than their *contestants/ competitors* on their way to the top.

3 The ancient city of the Incas, Machu Picchu, limits the number of *visitors/passengers* to 2,000 per day in order to reduce damage.

4 Providing for the needs of every *member/participant* of the family can be very difficult.

5 It will be better for everyone if doctors can show concern for their *clients/patients* as well as treating them.

6 *Individuals/Humans* raised in an environment where everything is done for them may be too reliant on others.

Useful language: positive and negative comments

1 ⊙ Here are some examples of positive and negative comments made by IELTS candidates.
Match the beginning and end of each sentence.

1 The first advantage of international tourism
2 The benefits of computer use in education
3 One of the disadvantages of radio
4 The negative aspect of the freedom to express your own ideas
5 Another positive result of increasing visitor numbers

a are compelling.
b is that it brings in foreign currency.
c is that tourist attractions can be developed.
d is that it is only an audio source.
e is the fact that some people abuse this privilege.

2 Complete the sentences below, expressing your own ideas about some of the topics in the box, or others that interest you.

> cheap public transport   living in a village   studying abroad   access to the Internet
> large families   working for a large company   using credit cards   large supermarkets

1 The first disadvantage ...

2 The main benefit ...

3 The negative aspect ...

4 One of the advantages ...

5 Another negative result of ...

6 A major drawback ...

Action plan reminder

1 Look at Writing Task 2 below and answer these questions.

- How much of the task do you need to read?
- How long should you spend on this task?
- What must you include in your answer?
- What should you underline in the task?
- Do you have to agree with the opinion in the exam question?
- Will you lose marks if you copy the wording of the task exactly?

Before you write

2 Make notes before you begin to write your essay. What should your notes include?

After you write

3 Answer these questions.

- Should you spend time checking your essay when you have finished?
- Should you spend time rewriting your essay neatly?
- Which of the following should you check for?
  overall structure; paragraphing; clearly linked ideas; up-to-date information; clear handwriting; humour; formal or neutral style; subject–verb agreement; quotations from famous writers; spelling; capital letters at the beginning of sentences; verb tenses; your own habitual errors

 Page 54 *Test 1 Writing Task 2 Action plan*

You should spend about 40 minutes on this task.

Write about the following topic:

In the past, shopping was a routine domestic task. Many people nowadays regard it as a hobby.

To what extent do you think this is a positive trend?

Give reasons for your answer and include any relevant examples from your own knowledge or experience.

Write at least 250 words.

Advice

Do you know a word that means 'routine domestic task'?

Do people spend time shopping instead of taking part in other activities?

Is there a connection between changes to the way people shop and the economic situation?

 Before the exam, make sure you know how much space you use for 250 words, then you won't need to spend time counting during the exam.

Speaking Part 1

Review

1 What must you remember to take to the exam room?

2 What do you have to answer questions about?

3 Will the questions all be about the same topic?

4 Do you get a separate mark for Speaking Part 1?

Tip! You can use the preparation ideas in this test to help you when you practise other IELTS speaking tests.

◀ Page 55 *Test 1 Speaking Part 1*

Useful language: work and studying

 Correct the one or two mistakes in these sentences written by IELTS candidates.

1 I went to Canada for studying engineering.

2 I am learning history at university.

3 I would like study oversea.

4 I have been study English for half a year.

5 I have classes at the daytime and I work in the evening.

6 I have a part-time work in a restaurant.

7 I am hoping to get a good employment when I graduate.

8 I finish my work at five o'clock.

9 There are lots of foreign pupils at my university.

10 I want to gain a lot of money.

Useful language: tenses

1 Look at these questions about a job. Think about what tense you would use in the answer and underline the verbs that help you decide.

1 What is your job?

2 How long have you been working there?

3 What do you enjoy about your job?

4 What job did you want to do when you were a child?

5 Do you think you will do a different job one day?

2 Which question(s):

1 ask about now? What tense is used?

2 ask about the past? What tense will you use in your answer?

3 ask about the future? Think of three different ways of beginning an answer.

4 ask about a length of time? What tense is used?

Tip! Listen carefully to the tense in the question so you give the right kind of answer.

3 Look at the questions about work/studying on page 96 and answer them about yourself.

Useful language: food vocabulary

1 Think about a place where you like to go if you eat out. Tick (✓) the things below that are most important to you. Add any other reasons you could give for choosing a restaurant or a café.

delicious/tasty food	family run	vegetarian
reasonably priced	part of a chain	traditional recipes
fresh ingredients	home-made dishes	lively atmosphere
fast service	plenty of choice	

Tip! If you never eat in a restaurant, imagine one where you would like to eat. You can do this in the test, too, if you don't have much personal experience of something.

2 Look at the questions about food and restaurants on page 96 and the Useful language below.

> Where I come from, …
> In my country we usually …
> When I'm at home, …
> Compared to my parents, …
> Until I came here, I …
> If I have something to celebrate, …
> My favourite restaurant …

Tip! Add some details to each answer and try to use a range of grammatical structures and vocabulary.

3 Practise saying your answers. Record yourself answering the questions. Listen to what you said and think about how to improve it. Did you speak clearly? Did you use a range of grammatical structures and vocabulary?

Speaking Part 2

Review

1 What does the examiner give you?

2 How long do you have to make notes?

3 Where should you write your notes?

4 How long do you talk for?

 Page 57 *Test 1 Speaking Part 2*

STRATEGIES

Making notes: spider diagrams

1 Look at this exam task and the completed spider diagram on the next page.

> **Describe your favourite TV programme.**
> **You should say:**
> > **the name of the programme and where it is set**
> > **what kind of programme it is**
> > **what it is about**
> **and explain why you enjoy it.**

Tip! Read the card carefully. Make sure you keep to the topic.

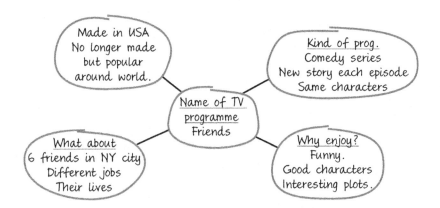

2 Now look at the task about a film on page 96 and write similar notes on the spider diagram below.

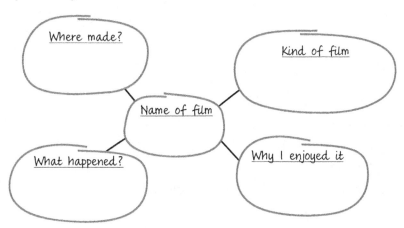

Useful language: giving a talk

1 Use your notes and record yourself talking about a film for two minutes. Use a clock.

> For me, the best part was ...
> It was one of the best films I've seen because of ...
> What stood out for me was ...
> I particularly liked ...
> Compared to other films, I felt ...

Tip! Although it doesn't matter what order you give the information asked for, make sure that what you say is logical.

2 Listen to what you said and think about how to improve it. Think about these questions.

Did you introduce the topic?

Did you use the correct tenses?

Did you use a range of vocabulary?

Did you connect your sentences?

Did you cover all the points on the card (not necessarily in that order)?

Did you speak clearly?

3 Look at the two follow-up questions on page 96 and think of your answers.

Speaking Part 3

Review

1 Will the questions be about a new topic?

2 Will they be about your own personal experience?

◄ **Page 59** *Test 1 Speaking Part 3*

Useful language: starting sentences with *-ing*

1 ⊘ People often start sentences with the *-ing* form when they want to make a general point about an activity. Rewrite these sentences so they begin with an *-ing* word.

  1 More effort is required to read than watch TV.
    Reading requires more effort than watching TV.

  2 The best way to learn is by doing, especially with children.
    .... works best, especially with children.

  3 It improves people's level of confidence if they do some kind of paid work.
    .... improves people's level of confidence.

  4 The most important thing for children is that they are loved.
    .... the most important thing for children.

  5 People can suffer from stress when they are faced with a lot of financial problems.
    .... a lot of financial problems can be very stressful.

  6 It is still considered a luxury to own a car in some parts of the world.
    .... is still considered a luxury in some parts of the world.

2 Finish these sentences about films.

  1 Going to the cinema nowadays is ....

  2 Watching a lot of violent films can ....

  3 Invading the privacy of film stars ....

  4 Watching films in English ....

3 Look at the questions on page 96 about films and the cinema and think about what you would say. Practise saying your answers.

Useful language: talking about the future

Do you agree with the statements below? Use an expression from the box with each statement to give your opinion.

It's likely that ...	It's doubtful whether ...
It seems probable that ...	I feel it's unlikely that ...
I'm not sure whether ...	I'd say that ...
I'm fairly certain that ...	I cannot imagine that ...

1 People will always enjoy occasional visits to the cinema rather than watch films at home.

2 The international film industry will continue to be dominated by the USA.

3 Watching films will become more popular than watching other kinds of programme on TV.

4 Less money will be available to the film industry.

5 There will be more computer-animated films.

6 More films will be made which have a family appeal.

7 Film stars will earn less money in future.

Useful language: making general statements

Answer these questions by making a general statement followed by your own opinion.

Tip! It is a good idea to talk about general opinions before giving your own.

1 Do you think fashion plays too big a part in our lives today?

2 How can tourism help people to understand other cultures?

3 Are people in your country interested in recycling?

4 How likely is it that people will stop reading books in the future?

General statement	Your opinion
For the most part, ...	but in fact ...
In general, ...	but I (don't) think ...
It's widely acknowledged that ...	but in my experience ...
Most people recognise that ...	but in my country ...
That depends.	and I agree that ...
That can vary according to the situation.	and because of that ...
In some circumstances, ...	For instance, I have noticed that ...
For some people ...	However, I believe ...

Speaking Part 1

The examiner will ask you some questions about yourself.

 Tip! Speak clearly. You will be marked on your pronunciation and how easy you are to understand.

Let's talk about your studies (or your job).

Are you a full-time student at the moment?
Where do you study?
How long have you studied there?
Is it far from your home?
What job would you like to have in the future?

OR

What is your job?
How long have you been working there?
What do you enjoy about your job?
What job did you want to do when you were a child?
Do you think you will do a different job one day?

The examiner will then ask you some questions about one or two other topics, for example:

Now let's talk about food and restaurants.

Do you often eat out in restaurants, cafés and so on?
How do you choose where to go when you want to eat out?
Are fast-food restaurants such as burger bars popular in your country?
Do you ever cook for yourself, or other people?
Can you recommend a restaurant in your home town?

Speaking Part 2

The examiner will give you a topic on a card like the one on the right and ask you to talk about it for one to two minutes. Before you talk you have one minute to think about what you're going to say. The examiner will give you some paper and a pencil so you can make notes if you want to.

The examiner may ask one or two more questions when you have finished, for example:

Do you often go to the cinema?
Do you think watching films in English is useful?

> **Describe a film you enjoyed.**
> **You should say:**
> **the name of the film and where it was made**
> **what kind of film it was**
> **what happened in the film**
> **and explain why you enjoyed it.**

Speaking Part 3

The examiner will ask some more general questions which follow on from the topic in Part 2.

Is going to the cinema more or less popular than it used to be, do you think?
What are the most popular types of film among people you know?
Do you think there's too much violence in films?
Should there be more films made for children?
Do films influence other things – fashion, for example?
Do you think the media invade the privacy of film stars or put them under too much pressure?
Do you think films will continue to be an important form of entertainment?

Tip! If you don't understand what you have to talk about, the examiner can rephrase it for you.

Tip! The examiner will notice if you try to use an answer you have learnt by heart and you will lose marks.

CD 2 02 *Questions 1–10*

Complete the notes below.

*Write **NO MORE THAN TWO WORDS AND/OR A NUMBER** for each answer.*

Midbury Drama Club

Background

Example	*Answer*
club started in	.........1957.........

● prize recently won by **1** .... section

● usually performs **2** .... plays

Meetings

● next auditions will be on Tuesday, **3** ....

● help is needed with **4** .... and ....

● rehearsals take place in the **5** .... hall

● nearest car park for rehearsals is in Ashburton Road opposite

the **6** ....

Costs

● annual membership fee is **7** £.........................

● extra payment for **8** ....

Contact

● secretary's name is Sarah **9** ....

● secretary's phone number is **10** ....

(CD 2 03) Questions 11–15

*Choose the correct letter, **A**, **B** or **C**.*

11   What does the charity *Forward thinking* do?

      A   It funds art exhibitions in hospitals.
      B   It produces affordable materials for art therapy.
      C   It encourages the use of arts projects in healthcare.

12   What benefit of *Forward thinking's* work does Jasmine mention?

      A   People avoid going to hospital.
      B   Patients require fewer drugs.
      C   Medical students do better in tests.

13   When did the organisation become known as *Forward thinking*?

      A   1986
      B   in the 1990s
      C   2005

14   Where does *Forward thinking* operate?

      A   within Clifton city
      B   in all parts of London
      C   in several towns and villages near Clifton

15   Jasmine explains that the Colville Centre is

      A   a school for people with health problems.
      B   a venue for a range of different activities.
      C   a building which needs repairing.

Who can take part in each of the classes?

Write the correct letter **A**, **B** *or* **C** *next to questions 16–20.*

Class participants	
A	children and teenagers
B	adults
C	all ages

16   Learn Salsa!   ....

17   Smooth Movers   ....

18   Art of the Forest   ....

19   The Money Maze   ....

20   Make a Play   ....

04 *Questions 21–26*

Complete the flow-chart below.

*Choose **SIX** answers from the box and write the correct letter, **A–I**, next to questions 21–26.*

A	air quality
B	journey times
C	land use
D	leisure facilities
E	means of transport
F	parking facilities
G	number of pedestrians
H	places of employment
I	traffic flow

CITY CENTRE FIELD TRIP

Chose area of city to study

Did a survey of **21** .... in city centre to compare with old maps

22 .... was assessed in five key locations

Measured **23** .... twice a day

Researched **24** .... during one afternoon

Looked at official figures

Measured **25** .... in several locations.

Asked questions about **26** ....

Who will be responsible for each task?

A	Stefan
B	Lauren
C	both Stefan and Lauren

Write the correct letter next to questions 27–30.

27 draw graphs and maps   ....

28 choose photographs   ....

29 write report   ....

30 do presentation   ....

🎧 05 *Questions 31–35*

Complete the sentences below.

*Write **ONLY ONE WORD** for each answer.*

Manufacturing in the English Midlands

31 In the eighteenth century, the .... still determined how most people made a living.

32 In the ground were minerals which supported the many .... of the region.

33 Since the late sixteenth century the French settlers had made ....

34 In Cheshire .... was mined and transported on the river Mersey.

35 Potters worked in a few .... situated on the small hills of North Staffordshire.

🎧 05 *Questions 36–40*

Complete the notes below.

*Write **ONE WORD** for each answer.*

Pottery notes

Earthenware

advantages:

- potters used **36** .... clay
- saved money on **37** ....

disadvantages:

- needed two firings in the kiln to be **38** ....
- fragility led to high **39** .... during manufacturing

Stoneware

- more expensive but better
- made from a **40** .... of clay and flint

*You should spend about 20 minutes on **Questions 1–13**, which are based on Reading Passage 1 below.*

Seed vault guards resources for the future

Fiona Harvey paid a visit to a building whose contents are very precious.

About 1,000 km from the North Pole, Svalbard is one of the most remote places on earth. For this reason, it is the site of a vault that will safeguard a priceless component of our common heritage – the seeds of our staple crops. Here, seeds from the world's most vital food crops will be locked away for hundreds or even thousands of years. If something goes wrong in the world, the vault will provide the means to restore farming. We, or our descendants, will not have to retread thousands of years of agriculture from scratch.

Deep in the vault at the end of a long tunnel, are three storage vaults which are lined with insulated panels to help maintain the cold temperatures. Electronic transmitters linked to a satellite system monitor temperature, etc. and pass the information back to the appropriate authorities at Longyearbyen and the Nordic Gene Bank which provide the technical information for managing the seed vaults. The seeds are placed in sealed boxes and stored on shelves in the vaults. The minimal moisture level and low temperature ensure low metabolic activity. The remote location, as well as the rugged structure, provide unparalleled security for the world's agricultural heritage.

The three vaults are buried deep in the hillside. To reach them, it is necessary to proceed down a long and surprisingly large corridor. At 93.3 metres in length, it connects the 26-metre long entrance building to the three vaults, each of which extends a further 27 metres into the mountain. Towards the end of this tunnel, after about 80 metres, there are several small rooms on the right-hand side. One is a transformer room to which only the power company officials have access – this houses the equipment needed to transform the incoming electrical current down to 220 volts. A second is an electrical room housing controls for the compressor and other equipment. The other room is an office which can be heated to provide comfortable working conditions for those who will make an inventory of the samples in and out of the vault.

Anyone seeking access to the seeds has to pass through four locked doors: the heavy steel entrance doors, a second door approximately 90 metres down the tunnel and finally the two keyed doors separated by an airlock, from which it is possible to proceed directly into the seed vaults. Keys are coded to allow access to different levels of the facility.

A work of art will make the vault visible for miles around. The vault entrance is filled with highly reflective sheets of steel and mirrors which form an installation acting as a beacon. It reflects polar light in the summer months, while in the winter, a network of 200 fibre-optic cables will give the piece a muted greenish-turquoise and white light.

Cary Fowler, the mastermind behind the vault, stands inside the echoing cavern. For him, this is the culmination of nearly 30 years of work. 'It's an insurance policy,' he explains, 'a very cheap insurance policy when you consider what we're insuring – the earth's biological diversity.'

Seeds are being brought here from all over the world, from seed banks created by governments, universities and private institutions. Soon, there will be seed varieties from at least 100 crops in the Svalbard vault – extending to examples of all of the 1.5 million known crop seed varieties in the world. If any more are unearthed, either in the wild or found in obscure collections, they can be added, too – the vault has room for at least 4.5 million samples.

Inside the entrance area it is more than 10° C below freezing, but in the chambers where the seeds are kept, refrigerators push down the temperature even further, to –18° C. At this temperature, which will be kept constant to stop the seeds germinating or rotting, the wheat seeds will remain viable for an estimated 1,700 years, the barley for 2,000 years and the sorghum for 20,000 years.

Svalbard's Arctic conditions will keep the seeds cold. In order to maintain the temperature at a constant –10° C to –20° C, the cold Arctic air will be drawn into the vault during the winter, automatically and without human intervention. The surrounding rock will maintain the temperature requirements during the extremely cold season and, during warmer periods, refrigeration equipment will engage. Looking out across the snow-covered mountains of Svalbard, it is hard not to feel respect for the 2,300 or so people who live here, mainly in Longyearbyen, a village a few miles away. There are three months without light in winter.

Svalbard is intended as the seed bank of last resort. Each sample is made up of a few hundred seeds, sealed inside a watertight package which will never be tampered with while it is in the vault. The packages of seeds remain the property of the collections they have come from. Svalbard will disburse samples 'only if all the other seeds in other collections around the world are gone,' explains Fowler. If seeds do have to be given out, those who receive them are expected to germinate them and generate new samples, to be returned to the vault.

Questions 1–6

Label the diagram below.

*Choose **NO MORE THAN TWO WORDS OR A NUMBER** from the passage for each answer.*

Write your answers in boxes 1–6 on your answer sheet.

The Svalbard Vault

The seeds are conserved by the cold and lack of **6** ....

The entrance to the seed vault itself is protected with doors with **5** .... between them.

The **4** .... is reduced as it enters the vault.

Seeds are processed in the **3** .... before they go into the vault.

A tunnel, which is **2** .... long, connects the entrance building to the vault.

The installation in the entrance consists of **1** .... and metal panels which maximise natural light.

Questions 7–13

Do the following statements agree with the information given in Reading Passage 1?

In boxes 7–13 on your answer sheet, write

TRUE	*if the statement agrees with the information*
FALSE	*if the statement contradicts the information*
NOT GIVEN	*if there is no information on this*

7   The vault has the capacity to accommodate undiscovered types of seed at a later date.

8   There are different levels of refrigeration according to the kinds of seeds stored.

9   During winter, the flow of air entering the vault is regularly monitored by staff.

10   There is a back-up refrigeration system ready to be switched on if the present one fails.

11   The people who work at Svalbard are mainly locals.

12   Once a seed package is in the vault, it remains unopened.

13   If seeds are sent from Svalbard to other banks, there is an obligation for the recipient to send replacements back.

*You should spend about 20 minutes on **Questions 14–26**, which are based on Reading Passage 2 below.*

WHAT COOKBOOKS REALLY TEACH US

A Shelves bend under their weight of cookery books. Even a medium-sized bookshop contains many more recipes than one person could hope to cook in a lifetime. Although the recipes in one book are often similar to those in another, their presentation varies wildly, from an array of vegetarian cookbooks to instructions on cooking the food that historical figures might have eaten. The reason for this abundance is that cookbooks promise to bring about a kind of domestic transformation for the user. The daily routine can be put to one side and they liberate the user, if only temporarily. To follow their instructions is to turn a task which has to be performed every day into an engaging, romantic process. Cookbooks also provide an opportunity to delve into distant cultures without having to turn up at an airport to get there.

B The first Western cookbook appeared just over 1,600 years ago. *De re coquinara* (it means 'concerning cookery') is attributed to a Roman gourmet named Apicius. It is probably a compilation of Roman and Greek recipes, some or all of them drawn from manuscripts that were later lost. The editor was sloppy, allowing several duplicated recipes to sneak in. Yet Apicius's book set the tone of cookery advice in Europe for more than a thousand years. As a cookbook it is unsatisfactory with very basic instructions. Joseph Vehling, a chef who translated Apicius in the 1930s, suggested the author had been obscure on purpose, in case his secrets leaked out.

C But a more likely reason is that Apicius's recipes were written by and for professional cooks, who could follow their shorthand. This situation continued for hundreds of years. There was no order to cookbooks: a cake recipe might be followed by a mutton one. But then, they were not written for careful study. Before the 19th century few educated people cooked for themselves. The wealthiest employed literate chefs; others presumably read recipes to their servants. Such cooks would have been capable of creating dishes from the vaguest of instructions.

D The invention of printing might have been expected to lead to greater clarity but at first the reverse was true. As words acquired commercial value, plagiarism exploded. Recipes were distorted through reproduction. A recipe for boiled capon in *The Good Huswives Jewell*, printed in 1596, advised the cook to add three or four dates. By 1653, when the recipe was given by a different author in *A Book of Fruits & Flowers*, the cook was told to set the dish aside for three or four days.

E The dominant theme in 16th and 17th century cookbooks was order. Books combined recipes and household advice, on the assumption that a well-made dish, a well-ordered larder and well-disciplined children were equally important. Cookbooks thus became a symbol of dependability in chaotic times. They hardly seem to have been affected by the English civil war or the revolutions in America and France.

F In the 1850s Isabella Beeton published *The Book of Household Management*. Like earlier cookery writers she plagiarised freely, lifting not just recipes but philosophical observations from other books. If Beeton's recipes were not wholly new, though, the way in which she presented them certainly was. She explains when the chief ingredients are most likely to be in season, how long the dish will take to prepare and even how much it is likely to cost. Beeton's recipes were well suited to her times. Two centuries earlier, an understanding of rural ways had been so widespread that one writer could advise cooks to heat water until it was a little hotter than milk comes from a cow. By the 1850s Britain was industrialising. The growing urban middle class needed details, and Beeton provided them in full.

G In France, cookbooks were fast becoming even more systematic. Compared with Britain, France had produced few books written for the ordinary householder by the end of the 19th century. The most celebrated French cookbooks were written by superstar chefs who had a clear sense of codifying a unified approach to sophisticated French cooking. The 5,000 recipes in Auguste Escoffier's *Le Guide Culinaire* (The Culinary Guide), published in 1902, might as well have been written in stone, given the book's reputation among French chefs, many of whom still consider it the definitive reference book.

H What Escoffier did for French cooking, Fannie Farmer did for American home cooking. She not only synthesised American cuisine; she elevated it to the status of science. 'Progress in civilisation has been accompanied by progress in cookery,' she breezily announced in *The Boston Cooking-School Cook Book*, before launching into a collection of recipes that sometimes resembles a book of chemistry experiments. She was occasionally over-fussy. She explained that currants should be picked between June 28th and July 3rd, but not when it is raining. But in the main her book is reassuringly authoritative. Its recipes are short, with no unnecessary chat and no unnecessary spices.

I In 1950 *Mediterranean Food* by Elizabeth David launched a revolution in cooking advice in Britain. In some ways *Mediterranean Food* recalled even older cookbooks but the smells and noises that filled David's books were not mere decoration for her recipes. They were the point of her books. When she began to write, many ingredients were not widely available or affordable. She understood this, acknowledging in a later edition of one of her books that 'even if people could not very often make the dishes here described, it was stimulating to think about them.' David's books were not so much cooking manuals as guides to the kind of food people might well wish to eat.

Questions 14–16

Complete the summary below.

Choose **NO MORE THAN TWO WORDS** from the passage for each answer.

Write your answers in boxes 14–16 on your answer sheet.

Why are there so many cookery books?

There are a great number more cookery books published than is really

necessary and it is their **14** .... which makes them differ from each

other. There are such large numbers because they offer people an escape

from their **15** .... and some give the user the chance to inform

themselves about other **16** ....

Questions 17–21

Reading Passage 2 has nine paragraphs, **A–I**.

Which paragraph contains the following information?

Write the correct letter, **A–I**, in boxes 17–21 on your answer sheet.
NB You may use any letter more than once.

17   cookery books providing a sense of stability during periods of unrest

18   details in recipes being altered as they were passed on

19   knowledge which was in danger of disappearing

20   the negative effect on cookery books of a new development

21   a period when there was no need for cookery books to be precise

Questions 22–26

Look at the following statements (**Questions 22–26**) and list of books (**A–E**) below.

Match each statement with the correct book, **A–E**.

Write the correct letter, **A–E**, in boxes 22–26 on your answer sheet.

22   Its recipes were easy to follow despite the writer's attention to detail.

23   Its writer may have deliberately avoided passing on details.

24   It appealed to ambitious ideas people have about cooking.

25   Its writer used ideas from other books but added additional related information.

26   It put into print ideas which are still respected today.

List of cookery books
A   *De re coquinara*
B   *The Book of Household Management*
C   *Le Guide Culinaire*
D   *The Boston Cooking-School Cook Book*
E   *Mediterranean Food*

*You should spend about 20 minutes on **Questions 27–40**, which are based on Reading Passage 3 below.*

Is there more to video games than people realise?

Many people who spend a lot of time playing video games insist that they have helped them in areas like confidence-building, presentation skills and debating. Yet this way of thinking about video games can be found almost nowhere within the mainstream media, which still tend to treat games as an odd mix of the slightly menacing and the alien. This lack of awareness has become increasingly inappropriate, as video games and the culture that surrounds them have become very big business indeed.

Recently, the British government released the Byron report into the effects of electronic media on children. Its conclusions set out a clear, rational basis for exploring the regulation of video games. The ensuing debate, however, has descended into the same old squabbling between partisan factions: the preachers of mental and moral decline, and the innovative game designers. In between are the gamers, busily buying and playing while nonsense is talked over their heads.

Susan Greenfield, renowned neuroscientist, outlines her concerns in a new book. Every individual's mind is the product of a brain that has been personalised by the sum total of their experiences; with an increasing quantity of our experiences from very early childhood taking place 'on screen' rather than in the world, there is potentially a profound shift in the way

children's minds work. She suggests that the fast-paced, second-hand experiences created by video games and the Internet may inculcate a worldview that is less empathetic, more risk-taking and less contemplative than what we tend to think of as healthy.

Greenfield's prose is full of mixed metaphors and self-contradictions and is perhaps the worst enemy of her attempts to persuade. This is unfortunate, because however much technophiles may snort, she is articulating widely held fears that have a basis in fact. Unlike even their immediate antecedents, the latest electronic media are at once domestic and work-related, their mobility blurring the boundaries between these spaces, and video games are at their forefront. A generational divide has opened that is in many ways more profound than the equivalent shifts associated with radio or television, more alienating for those unfamiliar with new technologies, more absorbing for those who are. So how do our lawmakers regulate something that is too fluid to be fully comprehended or controlled?

Adam Martin, a lead programmer for an online games developer, says: 'Computer games teach and people don't even notice they're being taught.' But isn't the kind of learning that goes on in games rather narrow? 'A large part of the addictiveness of games does come from the fact that as you play you are mastering a set of challenges. But humanity's larger understanding of the world comes primarily through communication and experimentation, through answering the question "What if?" Games excel at teaching this too.'

Steven Johnson's thesis is not that electronic games constitute a great, popular art, but that the mean level of mass culture has been demanding steadily more intellectual engagement from consumers. Games, he points out, generate satisfaction via the complexity of their virtual worlds, not by their robotic predictability. Testing the nature and limits of the laws of such imaginary worlds has more in common with scientific methods than with a pointless addiction, while the complexity of the problems children encounter within games exceeds that of anything they might find at school.

Greenfield argues that there are ways of thinking that playing video games simply cannot teach. She has a point. We should never forget, for instance, the unique ability of books to engage and expand the human imagination, and to give us the means of more fully expressing our situations in the world. Intriguingly, the video games industry is now growing in ways that have more in common with an old-fashioned world of companionable pastimes than with a cyber-future of lonely, isolated obsessives. Games in which friends and relations gather round a console to compete at activities are growing in popularity. The agenda is increasingly being set by the concerns of mainstream consumers – what they consider acceptable for their children, what they want to play at parties and across generations.

These trends embody a familiar but important truth: games are human products, and lie within our control. This doesn't mean we yet control or understand them fully, but it should remind us that there is nothing inevitable or incomprehensible about them. No matter how deeply it may be felt, instinctive fear is an inappropriate response to technology of any kind.

So far, the dire predictions many traditionalists have made about the 'death' of old-fashioned narratives and imaginative thought at the hands of video games cannot be upheld. Television and cinema may be suffering, economically, at the hands of interactive media. But literacy standards have failed to decline. Young people still enjoy sport, going out and listening to music. And most research – including a recent $1.5m study funded by the US government – suggests that even pre-teens are not in the habit of blurring game worlds and real worlds.

The sheer pace and scale of the changes we face, however, leave little room for complacency. Richard Bartle, a British writer and game researcher, says 'Times change: accept it; embrace it.' Just as, today, we have no living memories of a time before radio, we will soon live in a world in which no one living experienced growing up without computers. It is for this reason that we must try to examine what we stand to lose and gain, before it is too late.

Questions 27–32

Do the following statements agree with the views of the writer in Reading Passage 3?

In boxes 27–32 on your answer sheet, write

YES   *if the statement agrees with the views of the writer*
NO   *if the statement contradicts the views of the writer*
NOT GIVEN   *if it is impossible to say what the writer thinks about this*

27   Much media comment ignores the impact that video games can have on many people's lives.

28   The publication of the Byron Report was followed by a worthwhile discussion between those for and against video games.

29   Susan Greenfield's way of writing has become more complex over the years.

30   It is likely that video games will take over the role of certain kinds of books in the future.

31   More sociable games are being brought out to satisfy the demands of the buying public.

32   Being afraid of technological advances is a justifiable reaction.

Questions 33–37

*Choose the correct letter, **A**, **B**, **C** or **D**.*

*Write the correct letter, **A–D**, in boxes 33–37 on your answer sheet.*

33   According to the writer, what view about video games does Susan Greenfield put forward in her new book?

    A   They are exposing a child to an adult view of the world too soon.
    B   Children become easily frightened by some of the situations in them.
    C   They are changing the way children's view of the world develops.
    D   Children don't learn from them because they are too repetitive.

34   According to the writer, what problems are faced when regulating video games?

    A   The widespread and ever-changing use of games makes it difficult for lawmakers to control them.
    B   The appeal of the games to a younger generation isn't really understood by many lawmakers.
    C   The lawmakers try to apply the same rules to the games as they did to radio and television.
    D   Many lawmakers feel it is too late for the regulations to have much effect on the use of games.

35   What main point does Adam Martin make about video games?

    A   People are learning how to avoid becoming addicted to them.
    B   They enable people to learn without being aware of it happening.
    C   They satisfy a need for people to compete with each other.
    D   People learn a narrow range of skills but they are still useful.

36   Which of the following does Steven Johnson disagree with?

      A   the opinion that video games offer educational benefits to the user

      B   the attitude that video games are often labelled as predictable and undemanding

      C   the idea that children's logic is tested more by video games than at school

      D   the suggestion that video games can be compared to scientific procedures

37   Which of the following is the most suitable subtitle for Reading Passage 3?

      A   A debate about the effects of video games on other forms of technology.

      B   An examination of the opinions of young people about video games.

      C   A discussion of whether attitudes towards video games are outdated.

      D   An analysis of the principles behind the historical development of video games.

Questions 38–40

*Complete each sentence with the correct ending, **A–E**, below.*

*Write the correct letter, **A–E**, on your answer sheet.*

38   There is little evidence for the traditionalists' prediction that

39   A recent study by the US government found that

40   Richard Bartle suggests that it is important for people to accept the fact that

A	young people have no problem separating their own lives from the ones they play on the screen.
B	levels of reading ability will continue to drop significantly.
C	new advances in technology have to be absorbed into our lives.
D	games cannot provide preparation for the skills needed in real life.
E	young people will continue to play video games despite warnings against doing so.

Writing Task 1

You should spend about 20 minutes on this task.

The graph below gives information about international tourist arrivals in different parts of the world.

Summarise the information by selecting and reporting the main features, and make comparisons where relevant.

Write at least 150 words.

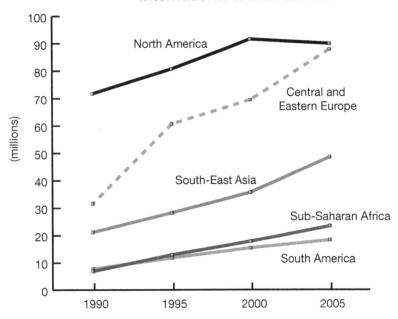

International tourist arrivals

Based on data published by the United Nations World Tourism Organization, 2008.

Writing Task 2

You should spend about 40 minutes on this task.

Write about the following topic:

Some people argue that it is more important to have an enjoyable job than to earn a lot of money. Others disagree and think that a good salary leads to a better life.

Discuss both these views and give your own opinion.

Give reasons for your answer and include any relevant examples from your own knowledge or experience.

Write at least 250 words.

Speaking Part 1

The examiner will ask you some questions about yourself, your home, work or studies and familiar topics.

Let's talk about your studies (or your job).
Are you studying or do you have a job?

Where are you studying?
How many hours do you spend there in a week?
Tell me something about the place where you study.
What are your favourite subjects?

OR

What is your job?
How long have you been doing that job?
Which part of your job do you enjoy the most? Why?
Tell me about the place where you work.

The examiner will then ask you some questions about one or two other topics, for example:

Now let's talk about your free time.
Do you spend a lot of time with your friends?
Do you go out much in the evening?
How much television do you watch?
Do you do any sports?

Speaking Part 2

The examiner will give you a topic on a card like the one on the right and ask you to talk about it for one to two minutes. Before you talk you'll have one minute to think about what you're going to say. The examiner will give you some paper and a pencil so you can make notes if you want to.

The examiner may ask one or two more questions when you have finished, for example:

Do you enjoy travelling?
Are you good at remembering things that happened a long time ago?

> **Describe a journey you remember well.**
> **You should say:**
>   **how you travelled**
>   **where you went**
>   **what happened**
> **and explain why the journey was**
> **memorable for you.**

Speaking Part 3

The examiner will ask some more general questions which follow on from the topic in Part 2.

Do you think too many people are dependent on cars as a means of transport?
Why do people prefer to travel by car? Is there a way of changing this attitude?
How could public transport systems be improved?
How can the amount of air travel be reduced throughout the world?
How will people travel in the future, do you think?

Questions 1–5

Complete the form below.

Write **ONE WORD AND/OR A NUMBER** *for each answer.*

MEGEQUIP CUSTOMER DETAILS

Example	*Answer*
Order from	..winter.. catalogue

Name   **1** .... Greening

Address   **2** .... York Terrace

Delivery address   5, York **3** ....

Payment method   **4** .... in advance

Reason for discount   address within the **5** ....

 Questions 6–10

Complete the table below.

Write **NO MORE THAN ONE WORD AND/OR A NUMBER** *for each answer.*

MEGEQUIP CUSTOMER ORDER				
Item	Catalogue no.	Catalogue section	Colour	Delivery notes
desk lamp	664	**6**	slate	customer will **7** ....
chair	131	Home Office	**8**	our van
filing cabinet two drawers with **9**	153	Commercial	grey	direct from London no later than **10** ....

CD2 07 *Questions 11 and 12*

*Choose **TWO** letters, **A–E**.*

Which **TWO** things make the museum unusual?

    A   the guides

    B   the events

    C   the animals

    D   the buildings

    E   the objects

CD2 07 *Questions 13 and 14*

*Choose **TWO** letters, **A–E**.*

Which **TWO** things can visitors do at the museum?

    A   buy home-made bread

    B   ride a horse

    C   ride on a tram

    D   buy copies of original posters

    E   go down a coal mine

Questions 15–20

Label the map below.

Write the correct letter, **A–I**, next to questions 15–20.

15	The exhibition centre	....
16	The High Street	....
17	The farmhouse	....
18	The coal mine	....
19	The Manor House	....
20	The Railway Station	....

Brampton open-air museum

CD2 08 *Questions 21–26*

Which attitude is associated with the following people during the conversation?

*Choose **SIX** answers from the box and write the correct letter, **A–H**, next to questions 21–26.*

Attitudes
A   amused
B   critical
C   forgetful
D   impatient
E   polite
F   relaxed
G   sympathetic
H   unrealistic

People

21   Cressida's fellow students   ....

22   Cressida   ....

23   Ainsley Webb   ....

24   Dr Erskine   ....

25   Professor Jenkins   ....

26   TV news centre staff   ....

Choose the correct letter, A, B or C.

27 What was Cressida asked to do at the beginning of her placement?

    A   go out to buy things for the production team
    B   run errands to other parts of the TV news centre
    C   meet visitors and escort them to the studio

28 What was fortunate for Cressida?

    A   She was familiar with a piece of equipment.
    B   She spent a lot of time in the editing suite.
    C   She was given a chance to interview someone.

29 What does Cressida feel she needs to improve?

    A   her understanding of business
    B   her organisational skills
    C   her ability to work in a team

30 What has given her an idea for her final assignment?

    A   a meeting with a public relations professional
    B   seeing a politician speaking to an audience
    C   a disagreement with one of the TV presenters

09 *Questions 31–40*

Complete the table below.

*Write **NO MORE THAN TWO WORDS** for each answer.*

THE HISTORY OF THE ELECTRIC GUITAR			
DATE	MAKER	NAME OF GUITAR	FEATURES
1890s	Orville Gibson	no name	similar in shape to a **31** ....
1925	John Dopyera	The National Guitar	made of metal, good for playing **32** .... music
1930s	C. F. Martin Company	The Dreadnought	strings made of **33** ....
1931	George Beauchamp	The **34**	used two **35** .... shaped like horseshoes to increase sound
1935	Adolph Rickenbacker	The Rickenbacker Electro Spanish	made from **36** ....
1941	Les Paul	The Log	the first to be completely **37** ....
1950	Leo Fender	The Fender Broadcaster	its simplicity made it ideal for **38** ....
1951	Leo Fender	The **39**	easy to carry around
1952	Ted McCarty	The Gibson Les Paul	**40** .... in colour
1954	Leo Fender	The Fender Stratocaster	double cutaway design

You should spend about 20 minutes on **Questions 1–13**, which are based on Reading Passage 1 below.

Can animals count?

Prime among basic numerical faculties is the ability to distinguish between a larger and a smaller number, says psychologist Elizabeth Brannon. Humans can do this with ease – providing the ratio is big enough – but do other animals share this ability? In one experiment, rhesus monkeys and university students examined two sets of geometrical objects that appeared briefly on a computer monitor. They had to decide which set contained more objects. Both groups performed successfully but, importantly, Brannon's team found that monkeys, like humans, make more errors when two sets of objects are close in number. 'The students' performance ends up looking just like a monkey's. It's practically identical,' she says.

Humans and monkeys are mammals, in the animal family known as primates. These are not the only animals whose numerical capacities rely on ratio, however. The same seems to apply to some amphibians. Psychologist Claudia Uller's team tempted salamanders with two sets of fruit flies held in clear tubes. In a series of trials, the researchers noted which tube the salamanders scampered towards, reasoning that if they had a capacity to recognise number, they would head for the larger number. The salamanders successfully discriminated between tubes containing 8 and 16 flies respectively, but not between 3 and 4, 4 and 6, or 8 and 12. So it seems that for the salamanders to discriminate between two numbers, the larger must be at least twice as big as the smaller. However, they could differentiate between 2 and 3 flies just as well as

between 1 and 2 flies, suggesting they recognise small numbers in a different way from larger numbers.

Further support for this theory comes from studies of mosquitofish, which instinctively join the biggest shoal* they can. A team at the University of Padova found that while mosquitofish can tell the difference between a group containing 3 shoal-mates and a group containing 4, they did not show a preference between groups of 4 and 5. The team also found that mosquitofish can discriminate between numbers up to 16, but only if the ratio between the fish in each shoal was greater than 2:1. This indicates that the fish, like salamanders, possess both the approximate and precise number systems found in more intelligent animals such as infant humans and other primates.

While these findings are highly suggestive, some critics argue that the animals might be relying on other factors to complete the tasks, without considering the number itself. 'Any study that's claiming an animal is capable of representing number should also be controlling for other factors,' says Brannon. Experiments have confirmed that primates can indeed perform numerical feats without extra clues, but what about the more primitive animals? To consider this possibility, the mosquitofish tests were repeated, this time using varying geometrical shapes in place of fish. The team arranged these shapes so that they had the same overall surface area and luminance even though they contained a different number of objects. Across hundreds of trials

* a group of fish

on 14 different fish, the team found they consistently discriminated 2 objects from 3. The team is now testing whether mosquitofish can also distinguish 3 geometric objects from 4.

Even more primitive organisms may share this ability. Entomologist Jurgen Tautz sent a group of bees down a corridor, at the end of which lay two chambers – one which contained sugar water, which they like, while the other was empty. To test the bees' numeracy, the team marked each chamber with a different number of geometrical shapes – between 2 and 6. The bees quickly learned to match the number of shapes with the correct chamber. Like the salamanders and fish, there was a limit to the bees' mathematical prowess – they could differentiate up to 4 shapes, but failed with 5 or 6 shapes.

These studies still do not show whether animals learn to count through training, or whether they are born with the skills already intact. If the latter is true, it would suggest there was a strong evolutionary advantage to a mathematical mind. Proof that this may be the case has emerged from an experiment testing the mathematical ability of three- and four-day-old chicks. Like mosquitofish, chicks prefer to be around as many of their siblings as possible, so they will always head towards a larger number of their kin. If chicks spend their first few days surrounded by certain objects, they become attached to these objects as if they were family. Researchers placed each chick in the middle of a platform and showed it two groups of balls of paper. Next, they hid the two piles behind screens, changed the quantities and revealed them to the chick. This forced the chick to perform simple computations to decide which side now contained the biggest number of its "brothers". Without any prior coaching, the chicks scuttled to the larger quantity at a rate well above chance. They were doing some very simple arithmetic, claim the researchers.

Why these skills evolved is not hard to imagine, since it would help almost any animal forage for food. Animals on the prowl for sustenance must constantly decide which tree has the most fruit, or which patch of flowers will contain the most nectar. There are also other, less obvious, advantages of numeracy. In one compelling example, researchers in America found that female coots appear to calculate how many eggs they have laid – and add any in the nest laid by an intruder – before making any decisions about adding to them. Exactly how ancient these skills are is difficult to determine, however. Only by studying the numerical abilities of more and more creatures using standardised procedures can we hope to understand the basic preconditions for the evolution of number.

Questions 1–7

Complete the table below.

*Choose **NO MORE THAN THREE WORDS** from the passage for each answer.*

Write your answers in boxes 1–7 on your answer sheet.

ANIMAL NUMERACY		
Subjects	**Experiment**	**Results**
Mammals and birds		
rhesus monkeys and humans	looked at two sets of geometrical objects on computer screen	performance of two groups is almost **1** ....
chicks	chose between two sets of **2** .... which are altered	chicks can do calculations in order to choose larger group
coots	behaviour of **3** .... birds was observed	bird seems to have ability to count eggs
Amphibians, fish and insects		
salamanders	offered clear tubes containing different quantities of **4**	salamanders distinguish between numbers over four if bigger number is at least two times larger
5	shown real shoals and later artificial ones of geometrical shapes; these are used to check influence of total **6** .... and brightness	subjects know difference between two and three and possibly three and four, but not between four and five
bees	had to learn where **7** .... was stored	could soon choose correct place

Questions 8–13

Do the following statements agree with the information given in Reading Passage 1?

In boxes 8–13 on your answer sheet, write

TRUE   *if the statement agrees with the information*
FALSE   *if the statement contradicts the information*
NOT GIVEN   *if there is no information on this*

8   Primates are better at identifying the larger of two numbers if one is much bigger than the other.

9   Jurgen Tautz trained the insects in his experiment to recognise the shapes of individual numbers.

10   The research involving young chicks took place over two separate days.

11   The experiment with chicks suggests that some numerical ability exists in newborn animals.

12   Researchers have experimented by altering quantities of nectar or fruit available to certain wild animals.

13   When assessing the number of eggs in their nest, coots take into account those of other birds.

Test 4 Reading Passage 2

*You should spend about 20 minutes on **Questions 14–26**, which are based on Reading Passage 2 below.*

Questions 14–18

Reading Passage 2 has five paragraphs **A–E**.

*Choose the correct heading for each paragraph, **A–E**, from the list of headings below.*

*Write the correct number, **i–viii**, in boxes 14–18 on your answer sheet.*

	List of Headings
i	A lack of consistent policy
ii	Learning from experience
iii	The greatest advantage
iv	The role of research
v	A unique material
vi	An irrational anxiety
vii	Avoiding the real challenges
viii	A sign of things to come

14 Paragraph **A**

15 Paragraph **B**

16 Paragraph **C**

17 Paragraph **D**

18 Paragraph **E**

Is it time to halt the rising tide of plastic packaging?

A Close up, plastic packaging can be a marvellous thing. Those who make a living from it call it a forgotten infrastructure that allows modern urban life to exist. Plastics have helped society defy natural limits such as the seasons, the rotting of food and the distance most of us live from where our food is produced. And yet we do not like it. Partly we do not like waste, but plastic waste, with its hydrocarbon roots and industrial manufacture, is especially galling. In 2008, the UK, for example, produced around two million tonnes of plastic waste, twice as much as in the early 1990s. The very qualities of plastic – its cheapness, its indestructible aura – make it a reproachful symbol of an unsustainable way of life. The facts, however, do not justify our unease. All plastics are, at least theoretically, recyclable. Plastic packaging makes up just 6 to 7 per cent of the contents of British dustbins by weight and less than 3 per cent of landfill. Supermarkets and brands, which are under pressure to reduce the quantity of packaging of all types that they use, are finding good environmental reasons to turn to plastic: it is lighter, so requires less energy for transportation than glass, for example; it requires relatively little energy to produce; and it is often re-usable. An Austrian study found that if plastic packaging were removed from the supply chain, other packaging would have to increase fourfold to make up for it.

B So are we just wrong about plastic packaging? Is it time to stop worrying and learn to love the disposable plastic wrapping around sandwiches? Certainly there are bigger targets for environmental savings such as improving household insulation and energy emissions. Naturally, the plastics industry is keen to point them out. What's more, concern over plastic packaging has produced a squall of conflicting initiatives from retailers, manufacturers and local authorities. It's a squall that dies down and then blows harder from one month to the next. 'It is being left to the individual conscience and supermarkets playing the market,' says Tim Lang, a professor specialising in food policy. 'It's a mess.'

C Dick Searle of the Packaging Federation points out that societies without sophisticated packaging lose half their food before it reaches consumers and that in the UK, waste in supply chains is about 3 per cent. In India, it is more than 50 per cent. The difference comes later: the British throw out 30 per cent of the food they buy – an environmental cost in terms of emissions equivalent to a fifth of the cars on their roads. Packagers agree that cardboard, metals and glass all have their good points, but there's nothing quite like plastic. With more than 20 families of polymers to choose from and then sometimes blend, packaging designers and manufacturers have a limitless variety of qualities to play with.

D But if there is one law of plastic that, in environmental terms at least, prevails over all others, it is this: a little goes a long way. This means, first, that plastic is relatively cheap to use – it represents just over one-third of the UK packaging market by value but it wraps more than half the total number of items bought. Second, it means that even though plastic encases about 53 per cent of products bought, it only makes up 20 per cent by weight of the packaging consumed. And in the packaging equation, weight is the main issue because the heavier something is, the more energy you expend moving it around. In view of this, righteous indignation against plastic can look foolish.

E One store commissioned a study to find precise data on which had less environmental impact: selling apples loose or ready-wrapped. Helene Roberts, head of packaging, explains that in fact they found apples in fours on a tray covered by plastic film needed 27 per cent less packaging in transportation than those sold loose. Steve Kelsey, a packaging designer, finds the debate frustrating. He argues that the hunger to do something quickly is diverting effort away from more complicated questions about how you truly alter supply chains. Rather than further reducing the weight of a plastic bottle, more thought should be given to how packaging can be recycled. Helene Roberts explains that their greatest packaging reduction came when the company switched to re-usable plastic crates and stopped consuming 62,000 tonnes of cardboard boxes every year. Plastic packaging is important, and it might provide a way of thinking about broader questions of sustainability. To target plastic on its own is to evade the complexity of the issues. There seems to be a universal eagerness to condemn plastic. Is this due to an inability to make the general changes in society that are really required? 'Plastic as a lightweight food wrapper is now built in as the logical thing,' Lang says. 'Does that make it an environmentally sound system of packaging? It only makes sense if you have a structure such as exists now. An environmentally driven packaging system would look completely different.' Dick Searle put the challenge another way. 'The amount of packaging used today is a reflection of modern life.'

Questions 19–23

Look at the following statements (Questions 19–23) and the list of people below.

Match each statement to the correct person **A–D**.

Write the correct letter, **A–D**, in boxes 19–23 on your answer sheet.

NB You may use any letter more than once.

19   Comparison of two approaches to packaging revealed an interesting result.

20   People are expected to do the right thing.

21   Most food reaches UK shops in good condition.

22   Complex issues are ignored in the search for speedy solutions.

23   It is merely because of the way societies operate that using plastic seems valid.

People	
A	Tim Lang
B	Dick Searle
C	Helene Roberts
D	Steve Kelsey

Questions 24–26

Complete the summary below.

Write **NO MORE THAN ONE WORD** from the text for each answer.

Write your answers in boxes 24–26 on your answer sheet.

A revolutionary material

Plastic packaging has changed the way we consume food. However, we instinctively dislike it, partly because it is the product of **24** .... processes, but also because it seems to be **25** .... so we feel it is wasteful. Nevertheless, it is thanks to plastic that for many people their choice of food is no longer restricted by the **26** .... in which it is available or the location of its source.

The growth of intelligence

No one doubts that intelligence develops as children grow older. Yet the concept of intelligence has proved both quite difficult to define in unambiguous terms and unexpectedly controversial in some respects. Although, at one level, there seem to be almost as many definitions of intelligence as people who have tried to define it, there is broad agreement on two key features. That is, intelligence involves the capacity not only to learn from experience but also to adapt to one's environment. However, we cannot leave the concept there. Before turning to what is known about the development of intelligence, it is necessary to consider whether we are considering the growth of one or many skills. That question has been tackled in rather different ways by psychometricians and by developmentalists.

The former group has examined the issue by determining how children's abilities on a wide range of tasks intercorrelate, or go together. Statistical techniques have been used to find out whether the patterns are best explained by one broad underlying capacity, general intelligence, or by a set of multiple, relatively separate, special skills in domains such as verbal and visuospatial ability. While it cannot be claimed that everyone agrees on what the results mean, most people now accept that for practical purposes it is reasonable to suppose that both are involved. In brief, the evidence in favour of some kind of general intellectual capacity is that people who are superior (or inferior) on one type of task tend also to be superior (or inferior) on others. Moreover, general measures of intelligence tend to have considerable powers to predict a person's performance on a wide range of tasks requiring special skills. Nevertheless, it is plain that it is not at all uncommon for individuals to be very good at some sorts of task and yet quite poor at some others.

Furthermore the influences that affect verbal skills are not quite the same as those that affect other skills.

This approach to investigating intelligence is based on the nature of the task involved, but studies of age-related changes show that this is not the only, or necessarily the most important, approach. For instance, some decades ago, Horn and Cattell argued for a differentiation between what they termed 'fluid' and 'crystallised' intelligence. Fluid abilities are best assessed by tests that require mental manipulation of abstract symbols. Crystallised abilities, by contrast, reflect knowledge of the environment in which we live and past experience of similar tasks; they may be assessed by tests of comprehension and information. It seems that fluid abilities peak in early adult life, whereas crystallised abilities increase up to advanced old age.

Developmental studies also show that the interconnections between different skills vary with age. Thus in the first year of life an interest in perceptual patterns is a major contributor to cognitive abilities, whereas verbal abilities are more important later on. These findings seemed to suggest a substantial lack of continuity between infancy and middle childhood. However, it is important to realise that the apparent discontinuity will vary according to which of the cognitive skills were assessed in infancy. It has been found that tests of coping with novelty do predict later intelligence. These findings reinforce the view that young children's intellectual performance needs to be assessed from their interest in and curiosity about the environment, and the extent to which this is applied to new situations, as well as by standardised intelligence testing.

These psychometric approaches have focused on children's increase in cognitive skills as they grow older. Piaget brought about a revolution in the approach to cognitive development through his arguments (backed up by observations) that the focus should be on the thinking processes involved rather than on levels of cognitive achievement. These ideas of Piaget gave rise to an immense body of research and it would be true to say that subsequent thinking has been heavily dependent on his genius in opening up new ways of thinking about cognitive development. Nevertheless, most of his concepts have had to be so radically revised, or rejected, that his theory no longer provides an appropriate basis for thinking about cognitive development. To appreciate why that is so, we need to focus on some rather different elements of Piaget's theorising.

The first element, which has stood the test of time, is his view that the child is an active agent of learning and of the importance of this activity in cognitive development. Numerous studies have shown how infants actively scan their environment; how they prefer patterned to non-patterned objects, how they choose novel over familiar stimuli, and how they explore their environment as if to see how it works. Children's questions and comments vividly illustrate the ways in which they are constantly constructing schemes of what they know and trying out their ideas of how to fit new knowledge into those schemes or deciding that the schemes need modification. Moreover, a variety of studies have shown that active experiences have a greater effect on learning than comparable passive experiences. However, a second element concerns the notion that development proceeds through a series of separate stages that have to be gone through step-by-step, in a set order, each of which is characterised by a particular cognitive structure. That has turned out to be a rather misleading way of thinking about cognitive development, although it is not wholly wrong.

Questions 27–30

*Choose the correct letter, **A**, **B**, **C** or **D**.*

Write your answers in boxes 27–30 on your answer sheet.

27 Most researchers accept that one feature of intelligence is the ability to

    A   change our behaviour according to our situation.
    B   react to others' behaviour patterns.
    C   experiment with environmental features.
    D   cope with unexpected setbacks.

28 What have psychometricians used statistics for?

    A   to find out if cooperative tasks are a useful tool in measuring certain skills
    B   to explore whether several abilities are involved in the development of intelligence
    C   to demonstrate that mathematical models can predict test results for different skills
    D   to discover whether common sense is fundamental to developing children's abilities

29 Why are Horn and Cattell mentioned?

    A   They disagreed about the interpretation of different intelligence tests.
    B   Their research concerned both linguistic and mathematical abilities.
    C   They were the first to prove that intelligence can be measured by testing a range of special skills.
    D   Their work was an example of research into how people's cognitive skills vary with age.

30   What was innovative about Piaget's research?

          A   He refused to accept that children developed according to a set pattern.

          B   He emphasised the way children thought more than how well they did in tests.

          C   He used visually appealing materials instead of traditional intelligence tests.

          D   He studied children of all ages and levels of intelligence.

Questions 31–36

Do the following statements agree with the views of the writer in Reading Passage 3?

In boxes 31–36 on your answer sheet, write

    YES   *if the statement agrees with the views of the writer*

    NO   *if the statement contradicts the views of the writer*

    NOT GIVEN   *if it is impossible to say what the writer thinks about this*

31   A surprising number of academics have come to the same conclusion about what the term intelligence means.

32   A general test of intelligence is unlikely to indicate the level of performance in every type of task.

33   The elderly perform less well on comprehension tests than young adults.

34   We must take into account which skills are tested when comparing intelligence at different ages.

35   Piaget's work influenced theoretical studies more than practical research.

36   Piaget's emphasis on active learning has been discredited by later researchers.

Questions 37–40

*Complete the summary using the list of words, **A–I**, below.*
*Write the correct letter, **A–I**, in boxes 37–40 on your answer sheet.*

Researchers investigating the development of intelligence have shown that **37** .... skills become more significant with age. One good predictor of **38** .... intelligence is the degree to which small children are **39** .... about their surroundings and how much interest they show on finding themselves in an **40** .... setting.

A	adult	**B**	practical	**C**	verbal
D	spatial	**E**	inquisitive	**F**	uncertain
G	academic	**H**	plentiful	**I**	unfamiliar

Writing Task 1

You should spend about 20 minutes on this task.

> *The graph below gives information about how much people in the United States and the United Kingdom spend on petrol.*
>
> *Summarise the information by selecting and reporting the main features, and make comparisons where relevant.*

Write at least 150 words.

How much do drivers spend on petrol?

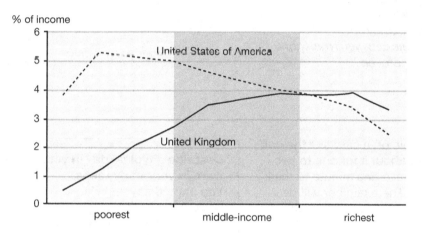

Writing Task 2

You should spend about 40 minutes on this task.

Write about the following topic:

> *It is generally believed that the Internet is an excellent means of communication but some people suggest that it may not be the best place to find information.*
>
> *Discuss both these views and give your own opinion.*

Give reasons for your answer and include any relevant examples from your own knowledge or experience.

Write at least 250 words.

Speaking Part 1

The examiner will ask you some questions about yourself, your home, work or studies and familiar topics.

Let's talk about your home town.

Where is your home town?
Can you describe the area you come from?
What facilities are there in your area for children/teenagers?
Is it a place where tourists go?

The examiner will then ask you some questions about one or two other topics, for example:

Now let's talk about how you travel.

How do you get to college/school/work?
Do you travel alone or with friends?
What do you do during your journey?
Do you ever have any problems with your transport?
How could your journey be improved?

Speaking Part 2

The examiner will give you a topic on a card like the one on the right and ask you to talk about it for one to two minutes. Before you talk you'll have one minute to think about what you're going to say. The examiner will give you some paper and a pencil so you can make notes if you want to.

The examiner may ask one or two more questions when you have finished, for example:

Do you like to have a routine to your day?
Do you like spending some time alone?

> **Describe a typical day in your life when you were in your early teens.**
> **You should say:**
> **what you did**
> **who you spent time with**
> **how you felt about the things you had to do**
> **and explain what was the best and worst part of the day for you.**

Speaking Part 3

The examiner will ask some more general questions which follow on from the topic in Part 2.

In what way is the relationship between parents and teenagers different from the relationship between parents and younger children?
What causes the most arguments between parents and teenagers?
Do teenagers have more independence in your country than they used to?
Who are the role models for teenagers in your country? Do you think they are good ones?

CD 3 02   *Questions 1–10*

Complete the notes below.

*Write **NO MORE THAN TWO WORDS AND/OR A NUMBER** for each answer.*

Costwise Car Hire

Example	Answer
Number of offices in Sydney:	...............3...............

Booking reference number: **1** ....

Office just by **2** .... terminal.

Opening hours: **3** .... to ....

After-hours charge: **4** $ ....

Cheapest model of car available: **5** ....

Information needed when booking: **6** .... number

Length of hire period: **7** ....

Reduce cost by driving under **8** .... km per week.

Insurance does not cover: **9** ....

After hours put keys in box near the office on the **10** ....

3 03 *Questions 11–15*

The following are essential requirements for which jobs?

*Write the correct letter, **A**, **B** or **C**, next to questions 11–15.*

Essential requirements
A foreign languages
B willingness to travel abroad
C professional qualification

11 conference organiser   ....

12 catering manager   ....

13 housekeeper   ....

14 fitness centre staff   ....

15 reservations assistant   ....

*Choose **FIVE** answers from the box and write the correct letter, **A–G**, next to questions 16–20.*

A	CV
B	names of referees
C	work permit
D	recruitment seminar
E	evidence of qualifications
F	conditions of employment
G	initial interview

INTERNATIONAL FINEST GROUP
RECRUITMENT PROCEDURES

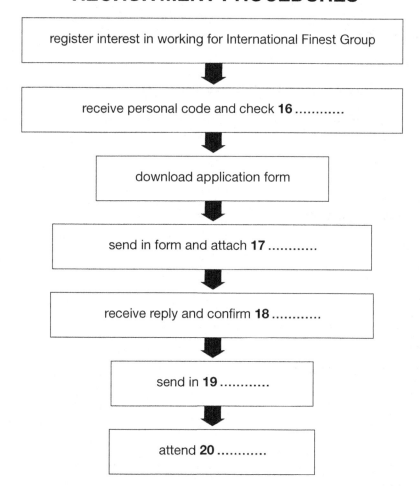

register interest in working for International Finest Group

⬇

receive personal code and check **16** ....

⬇

download application form

⬇

send in form and attach **17** ....

⬇

receive reply and confirm **18** ....

⬇

send in **19** ....

⬇

attend **20** ....

04 *Questions 21 and 22*

*Choose **TWO** letters, **A–E**.*

Which **TWO** possible objections to a roof garden are discussed?

    A   problems of access

    B   the cost of construction

    C   the time needed to install it

    D   who will look after it

    E   how to support the weight of it

04 *Questions 23 and 24*

*Choose **TWO** letters, **A–E**.*

Which **TWO** recent developments in roof-garden building are mentioned?

    A   waterproof barrier materials

    B   drainage systems

    C   tank designs

    D   lightweight construction materials

    E   watering systems

04 *Questions 25–30*

Label the diagram below.

*Write the correct letter, **A–H**, next to questions 25–30.*

25	wall	....
26	electric wire	....
27	fibre optic cable	....
28	wooden post	....
29	glass cap	....
30	acrylic rod	....

Light installation

(CD3 05) *Questions 31–36*

Complete the notes below.

*Write **NO MORE THAN TWO WORDS** for each answer.*

The Argus system

Developed by Rob Holman in N. Carolina with other researchers.

Research is vital for understanding of **31** ....

Matches information from under the water with information from a

32 .... According to S. Jeffress Williams, useful because can make

observations during a **33** ....

Dr Holman's sand collection

Dr H. has samples from every **34** ....

Used in teaching students of **35** ....

    e.g. US East Coast display:

    grains from south are small, light-coloured and **36** .... in shape

(CD3 05) *Questions 37–40*

Complete the flow-chart below.

*Write **NO MORE THAN THREE WORDS** for each answer.*

Taking samples when travelling

| to dig sand, a plastic or metal **37** .... is ideal | → | store in plastic bags | → | write date and place, using a **38** .... |

After reaching home

| log samples, noting location, including which part of beach | → | dry sample on **39** .... | → | transfer to container | → | add at least one **40** .... immediately |

*You should spend about 20 minutes on **Questions 1–13**, which are based on Reading Passage 1 below.*

NATURE ON DISPLAY IN AMERICAN ZOOS

by Elizabeth Hanson

The first zoo in the United States opened in Philadelphia in 1874, followed by the Cincinnati Zoo the next year. By 1940 there were zoos in more than one hundred American cities. The Philadelphia Zoo was more thoroughly planned and better financed than most of the hundreds of zoos that would open later but in its landscape and its mission – to both educate and entertain – it embodied ideas about how to build a zoo that stayed consistent for decades. The zoos came into existence in the late nineteenth century during the transition of the United States from a rural and agricultural nation to an industrial one. The population more than doubled between 1860 and 1900. As more middle-class people lived in cities, they began seeking new relationships with the natural world as a place for recreation, self-improvement, and spiritual renewal. Cities established systems of public parks, and nature tourism – already popular – became even more fashionable with the establishment of national parks. Nature was thought to be good for people of all ages and classes. Nature study was incorporated into school curricula, and natural history collecting became an increasingly popular pastime.

At the same time, the fields of study which were previously thought of as 'natural history' grew into separate areas such as taxonomy, experimental embryology and genetics, each with its own experts and structures. As laboratory research gained prestige in the zoology departments of American universities, the gap between professional and amateur scientific activities widened. Previously, natural history had been open to amateurs and was easily popularized, but research required access to microscopes and other equipment in laboratories, as well as advanced education.

The new zoos set themselves apart from traveling animal shows by stating their mission as education and the advancement of science, in addition to recreation. Zoos presented zoology for the non-specialist, at a time when the intellectual distance between amateur naturalists and laboratory-oriented zoologists was increasing. They attracted wide audiences and quickly became a feature of every growing and forward-thinking city. They were emblems of civic pride on a level of importance with art museums, natural history museums and botanical gardens.

Most American zoos were founded and operated as part of the public parks administration. They were dependent on municipal funds, and they charged no admission fee. They tended to assemble as many different mammal and bird species as possible, along with a few reptiles, exhibiting one or two specimens of each, and they competed with each other to become the first to display a rarity, like a rhinoceros. In the constant effort to attract the public to make return visits, certain types of display came in and out of fashion; for example, dozens of zoos built special islands for their large populations of monkeys. In the 1930s, the Works Progress Administration funded millions of dollars of construction at dozens of zoos. For the most part, the collections of animals were organised by species in a combination of enclosures according to a fairly loose classification scheme.

Although many histories of individual zoos describe the 1940s through the 1960s as a period of stagnation, and in some cases there was neglect, new zoos continued to be set up all over the country. In the 1940s and 1950s, the first zoos designed specifically for children were built, some with the appeal of farm animals. An increasing number of zoos tried new ways of organizing their displays. In addition to the traditional approach of exhibiting like kinds together, zoo planners had a new approach of putting animals in groups according to their continent of origin and designing exhibits showing animals of particular habitats, for example, polar, desert, or forest. During the 1960s, a few zoos arranged some displays according to animal behavior; the Bronx Zoo, for instance, opened its World of Darkness exhibit of nocturnal animals. Paradoxically, at the same time as zoo displays began incorporating ideas about the ecological relationships between animals, big cats and primates continued to be displayed in bathroom-like cages lined with tiles.

By the 1970s, a new wave of reform was stirring. Popular movements for environmentalism and animal welfare called attention to endangered species and to zoos that did not provide adequate care for their animals. More projects were undertaken by research scientists and zoos began hiring full-time vets as they stepped up captive breeding programs. Many zoos that had been supported entirely by municipal budgets began recruiting private financial support and charging admission fees. In the prosperous 1980s and 1990s, zoos built realistic 'landscape immersion' exhibits, many of them around the theme of the tropical rainforest and, increasingly, conservation moved to the forefront of zoo agendas.

Although zoos were popular and proliferating institutions in the United States at the turn of the twentieth century, historians have paid little attention to them. Perhaps zoos have been ignored because they were, and remain still, multi-purpose institutions, and as such they fall between the categories of analysis that historians often use. In addition, their stated goals of recreation, education, the advancement of science, and protection of endangered species have often conflicted. Zoos occupy a difficult middle ground between science and showmanship, high culture and low, remote forests and the cement cityscape, and wild animals and urban people.

Questions 1–7

Do the following statements agree with the information given in Reading Passage 1?

In boxes 1–7 on your answer sheet, write

> **TRUE**   if the statement agrees with the information
> **FALSE**   if the statement contradicts the information
> **NOT GIVEN** if there is no information on this

1   The concepts on which the Philadelphia zoo was based soon became unfashionable.

2   The opening of zoos coincided with a trend for people to live in urban areas.

3   During the period when many zoos were opened, the study of natural history became more popular in universities than other scientific subjects.

4   Cities recognised that the new zoos were as significant an amenity as museums.

5   Between 1940 and 1960 some older zoos had to move to new sites in order to expand.

6   In the 1970s new ways of funding zoos were developed.

7   There has been serious disagreement amongst historians about the role of the first zoos.

Questions 8–13

Complete the notes below.

Choose **NO MORE THAN ONE WORD** from the passage for each answer.

Write your answers in boxes 8–13 on your answer sheet.

- *Up to 1940*   More mammals and birds exhibited than **8** ....
  9 .... were very popular animals in many zoos at one time.

- *1940s and 1950s*   Zoos started exhibiting animals according to their
  10 .... and where they came from.

- *1960s*   Some zoos categorised animals by **11** ....

- *1970s*   **12** .... were employed following protests about animal care.

- *1980s onwards*   The importance of **13** .... became greater.

*You should spend about 20 minutes on **Questions 14–26**, which are based on Reading Passage 2 below.*

Can we prevent the poles from melting?

A growing number of scientists are looking to increasingly ambitious technological fixes to halt the tide of global warming. **Mark Rowe** reports.

A   Such is our dependence on fossil fuels, and such is the volume of carbon dioxide we have already released into the atmosphere, that most climate scientists agree that significant global warming is now inevitable – the best we can hope to do is keep it at a reasonable level, and even that is going to be an uphill task. At present, the only serious option on the table for doing this is cutting back on our carbon emissions, but while a few countries are making major strides in this regard, the majority are having great difficulty even stemming the rate of increase, let alone reversing it. Consequently, an increasing number of scientists are beginning to explore the alternatives. They all fall under the banner of geoengineering – generally defined as the intentional large-scale manipulation of the environment.

B   Geoengineering has been shown to work, at least on a small, localised scale, for decades. May Day parades in Moscow have taken place under clear blue skies, aircraft having deposited dry ice, silver iodide and cement powder to disperse clouds. Many of the schemes now suggested look to do the opposite, and reduce the amount of sunlight reaching the planet. One scheme focuses on achieving a general cooling of the Earth and involves the concept of releasing aerosol sprays into the stratosphere above the Arctic to create clouds of sulphur dioxide, which would, in turn, lead to a global dimming. The idea is modelled on historical volcanic explosions, such as that of Mount Pinatubo in the Philippines in 1991, which led to a short-term cooling of global temperatures by 0.5°C. The aerosols could be delivered by artillery, high-flying aircraft or balloons.

C   Instead of concentrating on global cooling, other schemes look specifically at reversing the melting at the poles. One idea is to bolster an ice cap by spraying it with water. Using pumps to carry water from below the sea ice, the spray would come out as snow or ice particles, producing thicker sea ice with a higher albedo (the ratio of sunlight reflected from a surface) to reflect summer radiation. Scientists have also scrutinised whether it is possible to block icefjords in Greenland with cables which have been reinforced, preventing icebergs from moving into the sea. Veli Albert Kallio, a Finnish scientist, says that such an idea is impractical, because the force of the ice would ultimately snap the cables and rapidly release a large quantity of frozen ice into the sea. However, Kallio believes that the sort of cables used in suspension bridges could potentially be used to divert, rather than halt, the southward movement of ice from Spitsbergen. 'It would stop the ice moving south, and local currents would see them float northwards,' he says.

D   A number of geoengineering ideas are currently being examined in the Russian Arctic. These include planting millions of birch trees: the thinking, according to Kallio, is that their white bark would increase the amount of reflected sunlight. The loss of their leaves in winter would also enable the snow to reflect radiation. In contrast, the native evergreen pines tend to shade the snow and absorb radiation. Using ice-breaking vessels to deliberately break up and scatter coastal sea ice in both Arctic and Antarctic waters in their respective autumns, and diverting Russian rivers to increase cold-water flow to ice-forming areas, could also be used to slow down warming, Kallio says. 'You would need the wind to blow the right way, but in the right conditions, by letting ice float free and head north, you would enhance ice growth.'

E   But will such ideas ever be implemented? The major counter-arguments to geoengineering schemes are, first, that they are a 'cop-out' that allow us to continue living the way we do, rather than reducing carbon emissions; and, second, even if they do work, would the side-effects outweigh the advantages? Then there's the daunting prospect of upkeep and repair of any scheme as well as the consequences of a

technical failure. 'I think all of us agree that if we were to end geoengineering on a given day, then the planet would return to its pre-engineered condition very rapidly, and probably within 10 to 20 years,' says Dr Phil Rasch, chief scientist for climate change at the US-based Pacific Northwest National Laboratory. 'That's certainly something to worry about. I would consider geoengineering as a strategy to employ only while we manage the conversion to a non-fossil-fuel economy.' 'The risk with geoengineering projects is that you can "overshoot",' says Dr Dan Lunt, from the University of Bristol. 'You may bring global temperatures back to pre-industrial levels, but the risk is that the poles will still be warmer than they should be and the tropics will be cooler than before industrialisation.'

F   The main reason why geoengineering is countenanced by the mainstream scientific community is that most researchers have little faith in the ability of politicians to agree – and then bring in – the necessary carbon cuts. Even leading conservation organisations believe the subject is worth exploring. As Dr Martin Sommerkorn, a climate change advisor says, 'But human-induced climate change has brought humanity to a position where it is important not to exclude thinking thoroughly about this topic and its possibilities despite the potential drawbacks. If, over the coming years, the science tells us about an ever-increased climate sensitivity of the planet – and this isn't unrealistic – then we may be best served by not having to start our thinking from scratch.'

Questions 14–18

Reading Passage 2 has six paragraphs, **A–F**.

Which paragraph contains the following information?

*Write the correct letter, **A–F**, in boxes 14–18 on your answer sheet. You may use any letter more than once.*

14 the existence of geoengineering projects distracting from the real task of changing the way we live

15 circumstances in which geoengineering has demonstrated success

16 maintenance problems associated with geoengineering projects

17 support for geoengineering being due to a lack of confidence in governments

18 more success in fighting climate change in some parts of the world than others

Questions 19–23

Complete the summary below.

*Choose **NO MORE THAN TWO WORDS** from the passage for each answer.*

Write your answers in boxes 19–23 on your answer sheet.

Geoengineering projects

A range of geoengineering ideas has been put forward, which aim either to prevent the melting of the ice caps or to stop the general rise in global temperatures. One scheme to discourage the melting of ice and snow involves introducing **19** .... to the Arctic because of their colour. The build-up of ice could be encouraged by dispersing ice along the coasts using special ships and changing the direction of some **20** .... but this scheme is dependent on certain weather conditions. Another way of increasing the amount of ice involves using **21** .... to bring water to the surface. A scheme to stop ice moving would use **22** .... but this method is more likely to be successful in preventing the ice from travelling in one direction rather than stopping it altogether. A suggestion for cooling global temperatures is based on what has happened in the past after **23** .... and it involves creating clouds of gas.

Questions 24–26

Look at the following people (Questions 24–26) and the list of opinions below.

Match each person with the correct opinion, **A–E**.

Write the correct letter, **A–E**, in boxes 24–26 on your answer sheet.

24 Phil Rasch

25 Dan Lunt

26 Martin Sommerkorn

List of opinions

A The problems of geoengineering shouldn't mean that ideas are not seriously considered.

B Some geoengineering projects are more likely to succeed than others.

C Geoengineering only offers a short-term solution.

D A positive outcome of geoengineering may have a negative consequence elsewhere.

E Most geoengineering projects aren't clear in what they are aiming at.

---

*You should spend about 20 minutes on **Questions 27–40**, which are based on Reading Passage 3 below.*

America's oldest art?

Set within treacherously steep cliffs, and hidden away in the secluded valleys of northeast Brazil, is some of South America's most significant and spectacular rock-art. Most of the art so far discovered from the ongoing excavations comes from the archaeologically-important National Park of the Serra da Capivara in the state of Piaui, and it is causing quite a controversy. The reason for the uproar? The art is being dated to around 25,000 or perhaps, according to some archaeologists, even 36,000 years ago. If correct, this is set to challenge the widely held view that the Americas were first colonised from the north, via the Bering Straits from eastern Siberia at around 10,000 BC, only moving down into Central and South America in the millennia thereafter.

Prior to the designation of 130,000 hectares as a National Park, the rock-art sites were difficult to get to, and often dangerous to enter. In ancient times, this inaccessibility must have heightened the importance of the sites, and indeed of the people who painted on the rocks. Wild animals and human figures dominate the art, and are incorporated into often-complex scenes involving hunting, supernatural beings, fighting and dancing. The artists depicted the animals that roamed the local ancient brushwood forest. The large mammals are usually painted in groups and tend to be shown in a running stance, as though trying to escape from hunting parties. Processions – lines of human and animal figures –

also appear of great importance to these ancient artists. Might such lines represent family units or groups of warriors? On a number of panels, rows of stylised figures, some numbering up to 30 individual figures, were painted using the natural undulating contours of the rock surface, so evoking the contours of the surrounding landscape. Other interesting, but very rare, occurrences are scenes that show small human figures holding on to and dancing around a tree, possibly involved in some form of a ritual dance.

Due to the favourable climatic conditions, the imagery on many panels is in a remarkable state of preservation. Despite this, however, there are serious conservation issues that affect their long-term survival. The chemical and mineral qualities of the rock on which the imagery is painted is fragile and on several panels it is unstable. As well as the secretion of sodium carbonate on the rock surface, complete panel sections have, over the ancient and recent past, broken away from the main rock surface. These have then become buried and sealed into sometimes-ancient floor deposits. Perversely, this form of natural erosion and subsequent deposition has assisted archaeologists in dating several major rock-art sites. Of course, dating the art is extremely difficult given the non-existence of plant and animal remains that might be scientifically dated. However, there are a small number of sites in the Serra da Capivara that are giving up their secrets through good systematic excavation. Thus, at Toca do Boqueirao da Pedra Furada, rock-art researcher Niéde Guidon managed to obtain a number of dates. At different levels of excavation, she located fallen painted rock fragments, which she was able to date to at least 36,000 years ago. Along with the painted fragments, crude stone tools were found. Also discovered were a series of scientifically datable sites of fireplaces, or hearths, the earliest dated to 46,000 BC, arguably the oldest dates for human habitation in the Americas.

However, these conclusions are not without controversy. Critics, mainly from North America, have suggested that the hearths may in fact be a natural phenomenon, the result of seasonal brushwood fires. Several North American researchers have gone further and suggested that the rock-art from this site dates from no earlier than about 3,730 years ago, based on the results of limited radiocarbon dating. Adding further fuel to the general debate is the fact that the artists in the area of the National Park tended not to draw over old motifs (as often occurs with rock-art), which makes it hard to work out the relative chronology of the images or styles. However, the diversity of imagery and the narrative the paintings create from each of the many sites within the National Park suggests different artists were probably making their art at different times, and potentially using each site over many thousands of years.

With fierce debates thus raging over the dating, where these artists originate from is also still very much open to speculation. The traditional view ignores all the early dating evidence from the South American rock-art sites. In a revised scenario, some palaeo-anthropologists are now suggesting that modern humans may have migrated from Africa using the strong currents of the Atlantic Ocean some 60,000 years or more ago, while others suggest a more improbable colonisation coming from the Pacific Ocean. Yet, while either hypothesis is plausible, there is still no supporting archaeological evidence between the South American coastline and the interior. Rather, it seems possible that there were a number of waves of human colonisation of the Americas occurring possibly over a 60,000–100,000 year period, probably using the Bering Straits as a land-bridge to cross into the Americas.

Despite the compelling evidence from South America, it stands alone: the earliest secure human evidence yet found in the state of Oregon in North America only dates to 12,300 years BC. So this is a fierce debate that is likely to go on for many more years. However, the splendid rock-art and its allied archaeology of northeast Brazil, described here, is playing a huge and significant role in the discussion.

Questions 27–29

Choose the correct letter, *A*, *B*, *C* or *D*.

Write the correct letter in boxes 27–29 on your answer sheet.

27   According to the first paragraph, the rock-art in Serra da Capivara may revolutionise accepted ideas about

      A   the way primitive people lived in North America.

      B   the date when the earliest people arrived in South America.

      C   the origin of the people who crossed the Bering Straits.

      D   the variety of cultures which developed in South America.

28   How did the ancient artists use the form of the rock where they painted?

      A   to mimic the shape of the countryside nearby

      B   to emphasise the shape of different animals

      C   to give added light and shade to their paintings

      D   to give the impression of distance in complex works

29   In the fourth paragraph, what does the writer say is unusual about the rock-artists of Serra da Capivara?

      A   They had a very wide range of subject-matter.

      B   Their work often appears to be illustrating a story.

      C   They tended to use a variety of styles in one painting.

      D   They rarely made new paintings on top of old ones.

Questions 30–36

In boxes 30–36 on your answer sheet, write

      YES   if the statement agrees with the claims of the writer

      NO   if the statement contradicts the claims of the writer

      NOT GIVEN   if it is impossible to say what the writer thinks about this

30   Archaeologists have completed their survey of the rock-art in Piaui.

31   The location of the rock-art suggests that the artists had a significant role in their society.

32   The paintings of animals show they were regarded as sacred by the ancient humans.

33   Some damage to paintings is most likely due to changes in the weather of the region.

34   The fact that some paintings were buried is useful to archaeologists.

35   The tools found near some paintings were probably used for hunting animals.

36   The North American researchers have confirmed Niéde Guidon's dating of the paintings.

Questions 37–40

Complete each sentence with the correct ending, *A–F*, below.

Write the correct letter, *A–F*, on your answer sheet.

37 Materials derived from plants or animals

38 The discussions about the ancient hearths

39 Theories about where the first South Americans originated from

40 The finds of archaeologists in Oregon

A	are giving rise to a great deal of debate among palaeo-anthropologists.
B	do not support the earliest dates suggested for the arrival of people in America.
C	are absent from rock-art sites in the Serra da Capivara.
D	have not been accepted by academics outside America.
E	centre on whether or not they are actually man-made.
F	reflect the advances in scientific dating methods.

Writing Task 1

You should spend about 20 minutes on this task.

The diagrams below give information about the manufacture of frozen fish pies.

Summarise the information by selecting and reporting the main features, and make comparisons where relevant.

Write at least 150 words.

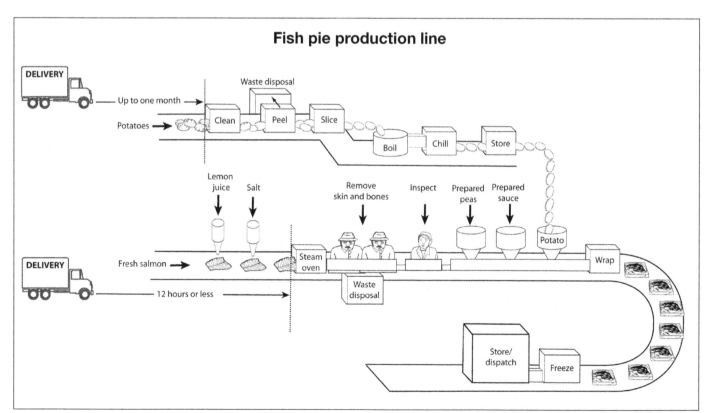

Writing Task 2

You should spend about 40 minutes on this task.

Write about the following topic:

> *In some countries it is thought advisable that children begin formal education at four years old, while in others they do not have to start school until they are seven or eight.*
>
> *How far do you agree with either of these views?*

Give reasons for your answer and include any relevant examples from your own knowledge or experience.

Write at least 250 words.

Speaking Part 1

The examiner will ask you some questions about yourself, your home,
work or studies and familiar topics.

Let's talk about your home town.

Do you live in a town or a city?
Have your family always lived there?
Do you like living there?
Do many tourists visit your area? (What do they come to see?)
Do you think your home town/city will change much in the future?

The examiner will then ask you some questions about one or two other topics, for example:

Now let's talk about music.

What kind of music do you like?
What do you like about it?
Are your friends interested in the same kind of music?
Where do you usually listen to music?
Do you ever go to concerts?
Do you play or would you like to play an instrument?

Speaking Part 2

The examiner will give you a topic on a card like the one on the
right and ask you to talk about it for one to two minutes. Before
you talk you'll have one minute to think about what you're going
to say. The examiner will give you some paper and a pencil so
you can make notes if you want to.

The examiner may ask one or two more questions when you
have finished, for example:

Do you throw things away when you don't need them any more?
Do you sometimes buy something and then regret it?

> **Describe one of your possessions which
> you couldn't live without.**
> **You should say:**
> > **what it is**
> > **why you first bought it / how you got it**
> > **when and how often you use it**
> **and explain why it is so special.**

Speaking Part 3

The examiner will ask some more general questions which follow on from the topic in Part 2.

Do you think some people spend too much money on things they don't need? What sort of things?
Is it worth trying to repair things which break rather than throwing them away? Why do you think that?
Many people feel they must have lots of hi-tech gadgets these days. What do you think of this trend?
Do you think technology has made our lives easier or more stressful? Why?
Some people aren't interested in keeping up to date with new technology. Do you think that matters?

Test 6 Listening Section 1 *Questions 1–10*

06 *Questions 1–10*

Complete the table below.

Write **ONE WORD AND/OR A NUMBER** *for each answer.*

HOSTELS			
Name	**Location**	**Cost of double room**	**Notes**
Hostelling International West End	*Example* 10 minutes from downtown by *Answer* .... bus	$50 per night but only $1 .... for members	Membership card offers discount on entry to 2 .... Internet access costs $3 per 3 ....
4 .... Hostel	Near beach. Two-minute walk to 5	$62. Meals extra but only available in 6	Was built as a hotel in 7 .... Can hire 8 .... from hostel
Backpackers Hostel	In 9 .... district	$45 plus $5 for breakfast	A 10 .... on every floor for guests to use

🎧 07 *Questions 11–15*

Label the map below.

*Choose **FIVE** answers from the box and write the correct letter, **A–H**, next to questions 11–15.*

A	biography
B	fiction
C	magazines
D	newspapers
E	non-fiction
F	photocopiers
G	reference books
H	study area

Choose the correct letter, A, B or C.

16   After two years, library members have to

      A   show proof of their current address.
      B   pay for a new membership card.
      C   bring a passport or identity card into the library.

17   What happens if you reserve a book?

      A   It will be available after five days.
      B   You can collect it a week later.
      C   You will be contacted when it is available.

18   Which materials can be borrowed for one week only?

      A   some reference books
      B   CD-ROMs
      C   children's DVDs

19   On which day does the library stay open later than it used to?

      A   Wednesday
      B   Saturday
      C   Sunday

20   Large bags should be left on the

      A   first floor.
      B   second floor.
      C   third floor.

08 *Questions 21–25*

Choose the correct letter, A, B or C.

21 Why did Anita and Lee choose to talk about John Chapman?

    A He was Lee's childhood hero.
    B They wanted to talk about the USA.
    C He was relevant to the topic of their studies.

22 Where did the students record their sources of information?

    A on their laptops
    B on a handout
    C on a database

23 The tutor claims she does not understand whether

    A apples grew in America before Europeans arrived.
    B the Native Americans had always eaten apples.
    C American apples were first bred in Europe.

24 The tutor says the audience was particularly interested to hear about

    A grafting techniques in ancient China.
    B the cultivation of apples in Kazakhstan.
    C the spread of apples along the Silk Route.

25 How will Anita and Lee present their follow-up work?

    A on the department website
    B as a paper
    C as a poster

08 *Questions 26–30*

What do Lee and Anita agree about their presentation skills with their tutor?

Write the correct letter, A, B or C, next to questions 26–30.

A excellent
B acceptable
C poor

Presentation skills

26 use of equipment   ....

27 handling software   ....

28 timing of sections   ....

29 design of handout   ....

30 clarity of speech   ....

09 *Questions 31–40*

Complete the table below.

*Write **NO MORE THAN ONE WORD** for each answer.*

INVESTIGATING TASTE		
Procedure	**Result**	**Cause**
more yellow added to green colour of **31**	subjects believed extra **32** .... added to drink	brain influenced by product presentation
gum chewed until it is **33** .... then again with sugar	mint flavour **34**	sweetness necessary for mintiness
same drink tasted cold and at room temperature	**35** .... drink seems sweeter	temperature affects sweetness
crisps eaten in rooms which were **36**	with louder crunch, subjects believed crisps taste **37**	sound affects taste perceptions
variety of cheese sauces prepared	subjects believed some sauces tasted less strong	**38** .... affects taste perceptions
two different flavoured **39** .... tasted together	subjects still tasted **40** .... when no longer there	brain is filling the taste 'gap'

*You should spend about 20 minutes on **Questions 1–13**, which are based on Reading Passage 1 below.*

Communicating in Colour

There are more than 160 known species of chameleons. The main distribution is in Africa and Madagascar, and other tropical regions, although some species are also found in parts of southern Europe and Asia. There are introduced populations in Hawaii and probably in California and Florida too.

New species are still discovered quite frequently. Dr Andrew Marshall, a conservationist from York University, was surveying monkeys in Tanzania, when he stumbled across a twig snake in the Magombera forest which, frightened, coughed up a chameleon and fled. Though a colleague persuaded him not to touch it because of the risk from venom, Marshall suspected it might be a new species, and took a photograph to send to colleagues, who confirmed his suspicions. *Kinyongia magomberae*, literally "the chameleon from Magombera", is the result, and the fact it was not easy to identify is precisely what made it unique. The most remarkable feature of chameleons is their ability to change colour, an ability rivalled only by cuttlefish and octopi in the animal kingdom. Because of this, colour is not the best thing for telling chameleons apart and different species are usually identified based on the patterning and shape of the head, and the arrangement of scales. In this case it was the bulge of scales on the chameleon's nose.

Chameleons are able to use colour for both communication and camouflage by switching from bright, showy colours to the exact colour of a twig within seconds. They show an extraordinary range of colours, from nearly black to bright blues, oranges, pinks and greens, even several at once. A popular misconception is that chameleons can match whatever background they are placed on, whether a chequered red and yellow shirt or a Smartie* box. But each species has a characteristic set of cells containing pigment distributed over their bodies in a specific pattern, which determines the range of colours and patterns they can show. To the great disappointment of many children, placing a chameleon on a Smartie box generally results in a stressed, confused, dark grey or mottled chameleon.

Chameleons are visual animals with excellent eyesight, and they communicate with colour. When two male dwarf chameleons encounter

*Smarties™ are sugar-coated chocolates in a range of bright colours.

each other, each shows its brightest colours. They puff out their throats and present themselves side-on with their bodies flattened to appear as large as possible and to show off their colours. This enables them to assess each other from a distance. If one is clearly superior, the other quickly changes to submissive colouration, which is usually a dull combination of greys or browns. If the opponents are closely matched and both maintain their bright colours, the contest can escalate to physical fighting and jaw-locking, each trying to push each other along the branch in a contest of strength. Eventually, the loser will signal his defeat with submissive colouration.

Females also have aggressive displays used to repel male attempts at courtship. When courting a female, males display the same bright colours that they use during contests. Most of the time, females are unreceptive and aggressively reject males by displaying a contrasting light and dark colour pattern, with their mouths open and moving their bodies rapidly from side to side. If the male continues to court a female, she often chases and bites him until he retreats. The range of colour change during female displays, although impressive, is not as great as that shown by males.

Many people assume that colour change evolved to enable chameleons to match a greater variety of backgrounds in their environment. If this was the case, then the ability of chameleons to change colour should be associated with the range of background colours in the chameleon's habitat, but there is no evidence for such a pattern. For example, forest habitats might have a greater range of brown and green background colours than grasslands, so forest-dwelling species might be expected to have greater powers of colour change. Instead, the males whose display colours are the most eye-catching show the greatest colour change. Their displays are composed of colours that contrast highly with each other as well as with the background vegetation. This suggests that the species that evolved the most impressive capacities for colour change did so to enable them to intimidate rivals or attract mates rather than to facilitate camouflage.

How do we know that chameleon display colours are eye-catching to another chameleon – or, for that matter, to a predatory bird? Getting a view from the perspective of chameleons or their bird predators requires information on the chameleon's or bird's visual system and an understanding of how their brains might process visual information. This is because the perceived colour of an object depends as much on the brain's wiring as on the physical properties of the object itself. Luckily, recent scientific advances have made it possible to obtain such measurements in the field, and information on visual systems of a variety of animals is becoming increasingly available.

The spectacular diversity of colours and ornaments in nature has inspired biologists for centuries. But if we want to understand the function and evolution of animal colour patterns, we need to know how they are perceived by the animals themselves – or their predators. After all, camouflage and conspicuousness are in the eye of the beholder.

Questions 1–4

Answer the questions below.

Choose **NO MORE THAN THREE WORDS** from the passage for each answer.

Write your answers in boxes 1–4 on your answer sheet.

1   What kind of climate do most chameleons live in?

2   Which animal caught a chameleon from an undiscovered species?

3   What was the new species named after?

4   Which part of the body is unique to the species *Kinyongia magomberae*?

Questions 5–13

Do the following statements agree with the information given in Reading Passage 1?

In boxes 5–13 on your answer sheet, write

>   **TRUE**   if the statement agrees with the information
>   **FALSE**   if the statement contradicts the information
>   **NOT GIVEN**   if there is no information on this

5   Few creatures can change colour as effectively as cuttlefish.

6   Chameleons can imitate a pattern provided there are only two colours.

7   Chameleons appear to enjoy trying out new colours.

8   Size matters more than colour when male chameleons compete.

9   After a fight, the defeated male hides among branches of a tree.

10   Females use colour and movement to discourage males.

11   The popular explanation of why chameleons change colour has been proved wrong.

12   There are more predators of chameleons in grassland habitats than in others.

13   Measuring animals' visual systems necessitates removing them from their habitat.

You should spend about 20 minutes on **Questions 14–26**, which are based on Reading Passage 2 below.

The Pursuit of Happiness

A

In the late 1990s, psychologist Martin Seligman of the University of Pennsylvania urged colleagues to observe optimal moods with the same kind of focus with which they had for so long studied illnesses: we would never learn about the full range of human functions unless we knew as much about mental wellness as we do about mental illness. A new generation of psychologists built up a respectable body of research on positive character traits and happiness-boosting practices. At the same time, developments in neuroscience provided new clues to what makes us happy and what that looks like in the brain. Self-appointed experts took advantage of the trend with guarantees to eliminate worry, stress, dejection and even boredom. This happiness movement has provoked a great deal of opposition among psychologists who observe that the preoccupation with happiness has come at the cost of sadness, an important feeling that people have tried to banish from their emotional repertoire. Allan Horwitz of Rutgers laments that young people who are naturally weepy after breakups are often urged to medicate themselves instead of working through their sadness. Wake Forest University's Eric Wilson fumes that the obsession with happiness amounts to a "craven disregard" for the melancholic perspective that has given rise to the greatest works of art. "The happy man," he writes, "is a hollow man."

B

After all, people are remarkably adaptable. Following a variable period of adjustment, we bounce back to our previous level of happiness, no matter what happens to us. (There are some scientifically proven exceptions, notably suffering the unexpected loss of a job or the loss of a spouse. Both events tend to permanently knock people back a step.) Our adaptability works in two directions. Because we are so adaptable, points out Professor Sonja Lyubomirsky of the University of California, we quickly get used to many of the accomplishments we strive for in life, such as landing the big job or getting married. Soon after we reach a milestone, we start to feel that something is missing. We begin coveting another worldly possession or eyeing a social advancement. But such an approach keeps us tethered to a treadmill where happiness is always just out of reach, one toy or one step away. It's possible to get off the treadmill entirely by focusing on activities that are dynamic, surprising, and attention-absorbing, and thus less likely to bore us than, say, acquiring shiny new toys.

C

Moreover, happiness is not a reward for escaping pain. Russ Harris, the author of *The Happiness Trap*, calls popular conceptions of happiness dangerous because they set people up for a "struggle against reality". They don't acknowledge that real life is full of disappointments, loss, and inconveniences. "If you're going to live a rich and meaningful life," Harris says, "you're going to feel a full range of emotions." Action toward goals other than happiness makes people happy. It is not crossing the finish line that is most rewarding, it is anticipating achieving the goal. University of Wisconsin neuroscientist Richard Davidson has found that working hard toward a goal, and making progress to the point of expecting a goal to be realised, not only activates positive feelings but also suppresses negative emotions such as fear and depression.

D

We are constantly making decisions, ranging from what clothes to put on, to whom we should marry, not to mention all those flavors of ice cream. We base many of our decisions on whether we think a particular preference will increase our well-being. Intuitively, we seem convinced that the more choices we have, the better off we will ultimately be. But our world of unlimited opportunity imprisons us more than it makes us happy. In what Swarthmore psychologist Barry Schwartz calls "the paradox of choice," facing many possibilities leaves us stressed out – and less satisfied with whatever we do decide. Having too many choices keeps us wondering about all the opportunities missed.

E

Besides, not everyone can put on a happy face. Barbara Held, a professor of psychology at Bowdoin College, rails against "the tyranny of the positive attitude". "Looking on the bright side isn't possible for some people and is even counterproductive," she insists. "When you put pressure on people to cope in a way that doesn't fit them, it not only doesn't work, it makes them feel like a failure on top of already feeling bad." The one-size-fits-all approach to managing emotional life is misguided, agrees Professor Julie Norem, author of *The Positive Power of Negative Thinking*. In her research, she has shown that the defensive pessimism that anxious people feel can be harnessed to help them get things done, which in turn makes them happier. A naturally pessimistic architect, for example, can set low expectations for an upcoming presentation and review all of the bad outcomes that she's imagining, so that she can prepare carefully and increase her chances of success.

F

By contrast, an individual who is not living according to their values, will not be happy, no matter how much they achieve. Some people, however, are not sure what their values are. In that case Harris has a great question: "Imagine I could wave a magic wand to ensure that you would have the approval and admiration of everyone on the planet, forever. What, in that case, would you choose to do with your life?" Once this has been answered honestly, you can start taking steps toward your ideal vision of yourself. The actual answer is unimportant, as long as you're living consciously. The state of happiness is not really a state at all. It's an ongoing personal experiment.

Questions 14–19

Reading Passage 2 has six paragraphs, **A–F**.

Which paragraph mentions the following?

*Write the correct letter, **A–F**, in boxes 14–19 on your answer sheet.*
NB *You may use any letter more than once.*

14   the need for individuals to understand what really matters to them

15   tension resulting from a wide variety of alternatives

16   the hope of success as a means of overcoming unhappy feelings

17   people who call themselves specialists

18   human beings' capacity for coping with change

19   doing things which are interesting in themselves

Questions 20 and 21

*Choose **TWO** letters, **A–E**.*

Write the correct letters in boxes 20 and 21 on your answer sheet.

Which **TWO** of the following people argue against aiming for constant happiness?

A	Martin Seligman
B	Eric Wilson
C	Sonja Lyubomirsky
D	Russ Harris
E	Barry Schwartz

Questions 22 and 23

Choose TWO letters, A–E.

Write the correct letters in boxes 22 and 23 on your answer sheet.

Which **TWO** of the following beliefs are identified as mistaken in the text?

A	Inherited wealth brings less happiness than earned wealth.
B	Social status affects our perception of how happy we are.
C	An optimistic outlook ensures success.
D	Unhappiness can and should be avoided.
E	Extremes of emotion are normal in the young.

Questions 24–26

Complete the sentences below.

*Choose **NO MORE THAN ONE WORD** from the passage for each answer.*

Write your answers in boxes 24–26 on your answer sheet.

24   In order to have a complete understanding of how people's minds work, Martin Seligman suggested that research should examine our most positive .... as closely as it does our psychological problems.

25   Soon after arriving at a .... in their lives, people become accustomed to what they have achieved and have a sense that they are lacking something.

26   People who are .... by nature are more likely to succeed if they make thorough preparation for a presentation.

The Deep Sea

At a time when most think of outer space as the final frontier, we must remember that a great deal of unfinished business remains here on earth. Robots crawl on the surface of Mars, and spacecraft exit our solar system, but most of our own planet has still never been seen by human eyes. It seems ironic that we know more about impact craters on the far side of the moon than about the longest and largest mountain range on earth. It is amazing that human beings crossed a quarter of a million miles of space to visit our nearest celestial neighbor before penetrating just two miles deep into the earth's own waters to explore the Midocean Ridge. And it would be hard to imagine a more significant part of our planet to investigate – a chain of volcanic mountains 42,000 miles long where most of the earth's solid surface was born, and where vast volcanoes continue to create new submarine landscapes.

The figure we so often see quoted – 71% of the earth's surface – understates the oceans' importance. If you consider instead three-dimensional volumes, the land-dwellers' share of the planet shrinks even more toward insignificance: less than 1% of the total. Most of the oceans' enormous volume, lies deep below the familiar surface. The upper sunlit layer, by one estimate, contains only 2 or 3% of the total space available to life. The other 97% of the earth's biosphere lies deep beneath the water's surface, where sunlight never penetrates.

Until recently, it was impossible to study the deep ocean directly. By the sixteenth century, diving bells allowed people to stay underwater for a short time: they could swim to the bell to breathe air trapped underneath it rather than return all the way to the surface. Later, other devices, including pressurized or armored suits, heavy metal helmets, and compressed air supplied through hoses from the surface, allowed at least one diver to reach 500 feet or so.

It was 1930 when a biologist named William Beebe and his engineering colleague Otis Barton sealed themselves into a new kind of diving craft, an invention that finally allowed humans to penetrate beyond the shallow sunlit layer of the sea and the history of deep-sea exploration began. Science then was largely incidental – something that happened along the way. In terms of technical ingenuity and human bravery, this part of the story is every bit as amazing as the history of early aviation. Yet many of these individuals, and the deep-diving vehicles that they built and tested, are not well known.

It was not until the 1970s that deep-diving manned submersibles were able to reach the Midocean Ridge and begin making major contributions to a wide range of scientific questions. A burst of discoveries followed in short order. Several of these profoundly changed whole fields of science, and their implications are still not fully understood. For example, biologists may now be seeing – in the strange communities of microbes and animals that live around deep volcanic vents – clues to the origin of life on earth. No one even knew that these communities existed before explorers began diving to the bottom in submersibles.

Entering the deep, black abyss presents unique challenges for which humans must carefully prepare if they wish to survive. It is an unforgiving environment, both harsh and strangely beautiful, that few who have not experienced it firsthand can fully appreciate. Even the most powerful searchlights penetrate only tens of feet. Suspended particles scatter the light and water itself is far less transparent than air; it absorbs and scatters light. The ocean also swallows other types of electromagnetic radiation, including radio signals. That is why many deep sea vehicles dangle from tethers. Inside those tethers, copper wires or fiber optic strands transmit signals that would dissipate and die if broadcast into open water.

Another challenge is that the temperature near the bottom in very deep water typically hovers just four degrees above freezing, and submersibles rarely have much insulation. Since water absorbs heat more quickly than air, the cold down below seems to penetrate a diving capsule far more quickly than it would penetrate, say, a control van up above, on the deck of the mother ship.

And finally, the abyss clamps down with crushing pressure on anything that enters it. This force is like air pressure on land, except that water is much heavier than air. At sea level on land, we don't even notice 1 atmosphere of pressure, about 15 pounds per square inch, the weight of the earth's blanket of air. In the deepest part of the ocean, nearly seven miles down, it's about 1,200 atmospheres, 18,000 pounds per square inch. A square-inch column of lead would crush down on your body with equal force if it were 3,600 feet tall.

Fish that live in the deep don't feel the pressure, because they are filled with water from their own environment. It has already been compressed by abyssal pressure as much as water can be (which is not much). A diving craft, however, is a hollow chamber, rudely displacing the water around it. That chamber must withstand the full brunt of deep-sea pressure – thousands of pounds per square inch. If seawater with that much pressure behind it ever finds a way to break inside, it explodes through the hole with laserlike intensity.

It was into such a terrifying environment that the first twentieth-century explorers ventured.

Questions 27–30

*Write the correct letter, **A**, **B**, **C** or **D**, in boxes 27–30 on your answer sheet.*

27 In the first paragraph, the writer finds it surprising that

    A   we send robots to Mars rather than to the sea bed.
    B   we choose to explore the least accessible side of the moon.
    C   people reached the moon before they explored the deepest parts of the earth's oceans.
    D   spaceships are sent beyond our solar system instead of exploring it.

28 The writer argues that saying 71% of the earth's surface is ocean is not accurate because it

    A   ignores the depth of the world's oceans.
    B   is based on an estimated volume.
    C   overlooks the significance of landscape features.
    D   refers to the proportion of water in which life is possible.

29 How did the diving bell help divers?

    A   It allowed each diver to carry a supply of air underwater.
    B   It enabled piped air to reach deep below the surface.
    C   It offered access to a reservoir of air below the surface.
    D   It meant that they could dive as deep as 500 feet.

30 What point does the writer make about scientific discoveries between 1930 and 1970?

    A   They were rarely the primary purpose of deep sea exploration.
    B   The people who conducted experiments were not professional scientists.
    C   Many people refused to believe the discoveries that were made.
    D   They involved the use of technologies from other disciplines.

Questions 31–36

Do the following statements agree with the views of the writer in Reading Passage 3?

In boxes 31–36 on your answer sheet, write

YES	*if the statement agrees with the views of the writer*
NO	*if the statement contradicts the views of the writer*
NOT GIVEN	*if it is impossible to say what the writer thinks about this*

31 The Midocean Ridge is largely the same as when the continents emerged.

32 We can make an approximate calculation of the percentage of the ocean which sunlight penetrates.

33 Many unexpected scientific phenomena came to light when exploration of the Midocean Ridge began.

34 The number of people exploring the abyss has risen sharply in the 21st century.

35 One danger of the darkness is that deep sea vehicles become entangled in vegetation.

36 The construction of submersibles offers little protection from the cold at great depths.

Questions 37–40

*Complete the summary using the list of words, **A–I**, below.*

Deep diving craft

A diving craft has to be **37** .... enough to cope with the enormous pressure of the
abyss, which is capable of crushing almost anything. Unlike creatures that live there, which are
not **38** .... because they contain compressed water, a submersible is filled with **39** ....
If it has a weak spot in its construction, there will be a **40** .... explosion of water into the craft.

A	ocean	**B**	air	**C**	deep
D	hollow	**E**	sturdy	**F**	atmosphere
G	energetic	**H**	violent	**I**	heavy

Writing Task 1

You should spend about 20 minutes on this task.

> *The charts below give information about weather in two Brazilian cities.*
>
> *Summarise the information by selecting and reporting the main features, and make comparisons where relevant.*

Write at least 150 words.

Rainfall

No. of wet days

■ average mm per month

Temperature

■ average daily high/low

Writing Task 2

You should spend about 40 minutes on this task.

Write about the following topic:

> *Some people choose to eat no meat or fish.*
>
> *They believe that this is not only better for their own health but also benefits the world as a whole.*
>
> *Discuss this view and give your own opinion.*

Give reasons for your answer and include any relevant examples from your own knowledge or experience.

Write at least 250 words.

Speaking Part 1

The examiner will ask you some questions about yourself, your home, work or studies and familiar topics.

Let's talk about your free time.

Do you have a lot of free time?
What do you like to do when you are at home?
Do you spend more time with your family or with friends?
Where do you go when you go out?
Is there enough to do in your home town?

The examiner will then ask you some questions about one or two other topics, for example:

Now let's talk about keeping fit.

Do you try to keep fit? How?
Do you think it's important for young people to keep fit?
Is sport compulsory for schoolchildren in your country?
Do you do any sports? Which do you like best?
Have you ever watched a sporting event live?

Speaking Part 2

The examiner will give you a topic on a card like the one on the right and ask you to talk about it for one to two minutes. Before you talk you have one minute to think about what you're going to say. The examiner will give you some paper and a pencil so you can make notes if you want to.

The examiner may ask one or two more questions when you have finished, for example:

Are you good at making decisions?
Do you think you usually make the right decisions?

> Describe an important decision you had to make.
> You should say:
>   what you had to decide
>   what or who helped you decide
>   if you made the right decision
> and explain why the decision was important.

Speaking Part 3

The examiner will ask some more general questions which follow on from the topic in Part 2.

Do you think it's harder to make decisions nowadays because we have so many choices?
What are the disadvantages of asking for other people's advice when making a decision?
Why do you think some people are better at making decisions than others?
Do you think children should be given the opportunity to make their own decisions? What kind of decisions?
Some people say we only learn by making mistakes. Do you agree?

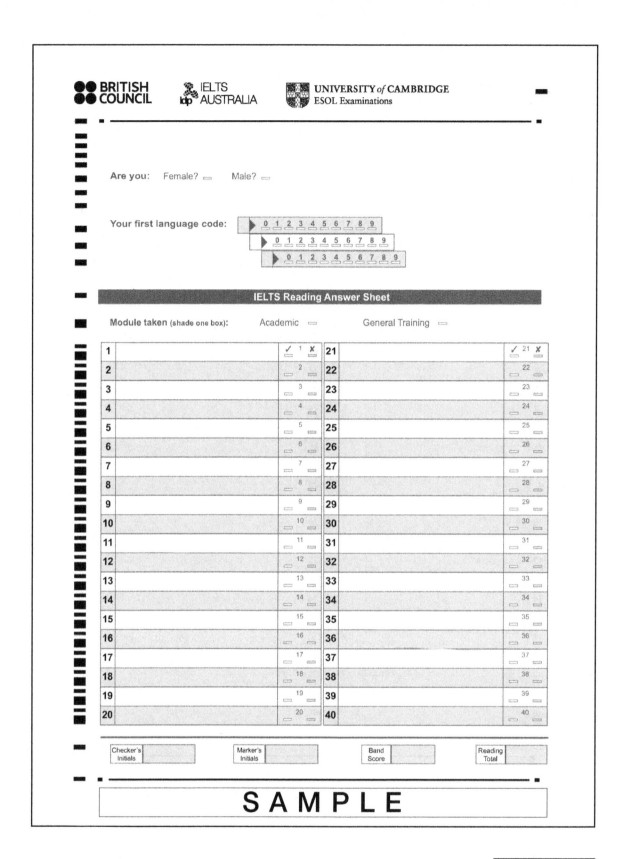

REPRODUCED WITH THE PERMISSION OF CAMBRIDGE ESOL

Photocopiable

Acknowledgements

The authors would like to thank Jane Coates for her efficient and patient editing, and Lynn Townsend, Annabel Marriott and Una Yeung at Cambridge University Press for all their encouragement and support. They would also like to thank Rowland Thomas, Christina Wylie and Ann Grubb for help with research. Many thanks also to Azadeh Hashemi for her help with the writing tasks and to Abbas Hashemi for patiently interpreting rough sketches. The authors and publishers are grateful to the staff and students of the Bell School, Cambridge, for their contributions to the writing exercises.

Development of this publication has made use of the Cambridge International Corpus (CIC). The CIC is a computerised database of contemporary spoken and written English which currently stands at over one billion words. It includes British English, American English and other varieties of English. It also includes the Cambridge Learner Corpus, developed in collaboration with the University of Cambridge ESOL Examinations. Cambridge University Press has built up the CIC to provide evidence about language use that helps to produce better language teaching materials.

The authors and publishers acknowledge the following sources of copyright material and are grateful for the permissions granted. While every effort has been made, it has not always been possible to identify the sources of all the material used, or to trace all copyright holders. If any omissions are brought to our notice, we will be happy to include the appropriate acknowledgements on reprinting.

Natural Environment Research Council for the text on p. 24 'Walking with Dinosaurs' by Peter Falkingham. *Planet Earth*, Spring 2009. Reproduced with permission; Penguin Books Ltd and Random House (US) for the text on pp. 29–30 'The robots are coming – or are they?' from *Physics of the Impossible: A Scientific Exploration into the World of Phasers, Force Fields, Teleportation and Time Travel* by Michio Kaku. (Allen Lane 2008). Copyright © Michio Kaku 2008. Reproduced by permission of Penguin Books Ltd and Doubleday, a division of Random House, Inc.; Peter Monaghan for the text on pp. 35–36 'Endangered languages' from 'Never mind the whales, save the languages', *The Australian*, 24.6.09. Reproduced with permission; Population Reference Bureau for adapted bar charts on p. 40 and p. 47 from *Population Bulletin*, Vol 62, no 3, 2007 and Vol 63, no 3, 2008. Reproduced with permission; National Geographic for the text on pp. 69–70 'Our Vanishing Night' by Verlyn Klinkenborg. *National Geographic*, November 2008. Reproduced with permission; The British Psychological Society for the text on pp. 74–75 'Is there a psychologist in the building?' written by Christian Jarrett, *The Psychologist*, October 2006. www.thepsychologist.org.uk. With permission from the British Psychological Society; New Scientist for the text on pp. 78–79 'Have teenagers always existed?' from 'Teenagers Special: The original rebels' written by Lynn Dicks, *New Scientist*, 5 March 2005, and for the text on pp. 122–123 'Can animals count?' from 'Animals that count' written by Ewen Callaway, *New Scientist*, 20 June 2009. Copyright © New Scientist Magazine; The University of Bristol for the adapted chart on p. 87 'The Young Ones, 100 years of Bristol's Students'. *Nonesuch* Summer 2009. Copyright © The University of Bristol; The Financial Times for the text on pp. 103–104 'Seed vault guards resources for the future' from 'In case of emergency, break ice' by Fiona Harvey, *The Financial Times*, 26 April 2008, and for the text on pp. 127–128 'Is it time to halt the rising tide of plastic packaging?' from 'Plastic: the elephant in the room' by Sam Knight, *The Financial Times*, 25 April 2008. Copyright © Financial Times Ltd; The Economist for the text on pp. 106–107 'What cookbooks really teach us' from 'Pluck a Flamingo', *The Economist*, 18 December 2008. Copyright © The Economist Newspaper Limited, London, 2008; Prospect Magazine for the text on pp. 110–111 'Is there more to video games than people realise?' from 'Rage against the machines' by Tom Chatfield, *Prospect Magazine*, 29 June 2008. Reproduced with permission; National Tax Journal for the table on p. 133 'How much do drivers spend on petrol?' from *The National Tax Journal*, June 1997, 50 (2), 233–259. Reproduced with permission; Princeton University Press for the text on pp. 140–141 'Nature on display in American Zoos' from *Animal Attractions*, written by Elizabeth Hanson. Copyright © Princeton University Press, 2002 and for the text on pp. 166–167 'The Deep Sea' from *The Eternal Darkness* written by Robert Ballard. Copyright © Princeton University Press and Robert Ballard, 2000. Reprinted by permission of Princeton University Press; Geographical magazine for the text on pp. 143–144 'Can we prevent the poles from melting?' from 'Can space mirrors save the planet?' written by Mark Rowe, *Geographical Magazine*, November 2009. Reproduced with permission; Current Publishing for the text on pp. 147–148 'America's oldest art?' written by George Nash, *Current Archaeology*, Issue 37. Reproduced with permission; Control Publications for part text on pp. 159–160 'Communicating in colour' written by Devi-Stuart Fox, *Australasian Science Magazine*, June 2008. Reproduced with permission; The Guardian for part text on pp. 159–160 'Communicating in colour' from 'Snake spits out new species of Chameleon at scientist's feet', by Esther Addley, *The Guardian*, 23 November 2009. Copyright © Guardian News & Media Ltd, 2009; Psychology Today for the text on pp. 162–163 'The Pursuit of Happiness' from *Psychology Today*, 15 December 2008; Rough Guides Ltd for the weather charts for Brasilia and Recife on p. 170 taken from *Rough Guide to Weather* by Robert Henson (Rough Guides 2002, 2007). Copyright © Robert Henson, 2002, 2007. Reproduced with permission of Rough Guides Ltd.

For permission to reproduce photographs:
Alamy/© Arcticphoto p. 103, /© Peter Alvey p. 127; Corbis/© Wayne Lynch/All Canada Photos p. 159; Photolibraryuk/© BildagenturShuster p. 69, /© Fabio Colombini Medeiros p. 147, /© Jeffrey L. Rotman p. 166
Illustrations: Abbas Hashemi pp. 20, 64, 138, 151; Janos Jantner pp. 26, 29, 105, 118

Audio recordings by John Green TEFL Audio. Engineer: Adam Helal; Editor: Tim Woolf; Producer: John Green. Recorded at ID Audio Studios, London.

Designed and typeset by eMC Design Ltd

CPSIA information can be obtained at www.ICGtesting.com
Printed in the USA
LVOW03s1051080115

421814LV00002B/3/P